Routledge Revivals

International Accounting

First published in 1985, *International Accounting: A Survey* by J.M. Samuels and A.G. Piper offers a comprehensive exploration of global accounting practices and their evolution. Covering topics such as harmonization, classification, and the international dimensions of financial reporting, the book examines the role of accounting in economic development and the spread of ideas across borders. With detailed references to international standards and study group publications, it remains an essential resource for understanding global accounting frameworks.

International Accounting

A Survey

J.M. Samuels and A. G. Piper

Routledge
Taylor & Francis Group

First published in 1985
by Croom Helm

This edition first published in 2026 by Routledge
4 Park Square, Milton Park, Abingdon, Oxon, OX14 4RN

and by Routledge
605 Third Avenue, New York, NY 10158

Routledge is an imprint of the Taylor & Francis Group, an informa business

Publisher's Note
The publisher has gone to great lengths to ensure the quality of this reprint but points out that some imperfections in the original copies may be apparent.

Disclaimer
The publisher has made every effort to trace copyright holders and welcomes correspondence from those they have been unable to contact.

For Product Safety Concerns and Information please contact our EU representative GPSR@taylorandfrancis.com. Taylor & Francis Verlag GmbH, Kaufingerstraße 24, 80331 München, Germany

A Library of Congress record exists under ISBN: 9780312419455

ISBN: 978-1-041-30073-1 (hbk)
ISBN: 978-1-003-77276-7 (ebk)
ISBN: 978-1-041-30076-2 (pbk)

Book DOI 10.4324/9781003772767

International Accounting: A Survey

J.M. Samuels
and A.G. Piper

This Work was commissioned by the Economic and Social Research Council as part of its accounting initiative.

CROOM HELM
London & Sydney

Croom Helm Ltd, Provident House, Burrell Row,
Beckenham, Kent BR3 1AT

Croom Helm Australia Pty Ltd, First Floor,
139 King Street, Sydney, NSW 2001, Australia

British Library Cataloguing in Publication Data

Samuels, J.M.
International accounting: a survey.
1. Accounting 2. International business
enterprises–Accounting
I. Title II. Piper, A.G. III. Economic
and Social Research Council
657 HF5657

ISBN 0-7099-3356-8

Printed and bound in Great Britain by
Biddles Ltd, Guildford and King's Lynn

CONTENTS

Chapter One

INTRODUCTION AND DEFINITION

a) Introduction

The 1980-81 International Accounting and Auditing Standards Committee of the AAA concluded that "the widely acknowledged importance of the international accounting and auditing fields is at present not adequately reflected in ....the quantity and quality of research". The Committee is critical of the research in this field, regarding much of it as dull, lacking a framework of reference, with few theoretical treatises and little scientific rigour in the empirical studies.

A survey of the literature does support this view. International accounting lags behind other aspects of accounting in the application of a rigorous approach to research. Up to the present time (the end of 1983) most of the articles on the subject have appeared in the professional literature rather than in research journals, and most of the books on the subject have been textbooks rather than research monographs. Not surprisingly therefore the articles on the subject are out of balance, with much of the work descriptive and showing an excessive concern with one aspect of the subject, namely harmonizing accounting practices, based not so much on theory and paradigms as on opinions. The research literature is however showing signs of improvement, with a number of scholarly articles appearing within the last five or so years. As a result of the increase in interest in the subject amongst academics and with the subject becoming a part of the curriculum in many universities, it is to be hoped that the good research articles become more frequent.

It can be argued that there is nothing new about international accounting. Indeed accounting has always been international. It is true that the literature emphasising this particular aspect of the subject mushroomed in the 1960s and 1970s, but from the time accounting emerged some thousands of years ago, it has always been international, both because of its concern with international trade and because of the spread of ideas across countries. Choi and Mueller (1979) state "The heritage of accounting is indisputably international. So today's concern with multinational accounting is more a renaissance than a new idea". Parker (1971) makes the same point; as a result of analysing important stages in the history of accounting, he emphasises that modern accounting is not the invention of any one country, and draws attention to the fact that it has always been international in its scope.

The increasing interest in the subject over the last two or three decades can be explained by a number of factors, one of the key ones being the desire of a number of interest groups to harmonize accounting across countries. It is often pointed out that business has become more international and that it would assist the free movement of capital and goods across frontiers if we had a common language of accounting. Mueller and Walker (1976) refer to the fact that "the dream of international standards for accounting, auditing and financial reporting has been with accountants for a long time". They believe it gained renewed momentum when Kraayenhof (1960) keynoted the urgency of establishing international standards at his plenary address to the 1959 annual meeting of the AICPA in San Francisco. The real breakthrough they believe came with the establishment of the IASC in June 1973.

Not all would agree with this view of the importance of the two events, but the dream referred to has certainly been an important factor leading to the current interest in the international aspect of the subject. The harmonization literature therefore forms an important aspect of this review.

Before that however, the spread of ideas is discussed, because as Kraayenhof said (1960), even if there is not agreement on an international set of rules, the "international exchange of views would be of incalculable value". This exchange of views, leading to the movement of accounting ideas from one country to another has a very long tradition. In the past the movement of ideas was very much slower than it is now. It was accomplished through the movement of people and through trade. In fact, it still is, there is nothing new about international trade, international business or the movement of scholars.

International accounting has, in the minds of some people, become synonymous with the move towards the harmonization of accounting across countries, with the possible uniformity of accounting practice. There is however very much more to the subject than that. The bi-lateral and multilateral discussions of accountants and the trend in business towards becoming more international, has led to an increasing interest in international accounting. Whether this exchange of views and greater understanding of the approach and attitudes of other countries will lead to harmonization does not matter. The spread of knowledge is itself valuable. Countries differ in so many respects; all those concerned with accounting benefit from knowing what is going on in other countries. Good ideas from wherever they come should be welcomed. This spread of ideas is as much international accounting as any other sub-division of the subject.

b) Defining International Accounting

International accounting is a loose term, it has no agreed definition. This is not really surprising as there are so many different aspects of accounting that have an international dimension. The literature identifies at least four areas:

i) the historical dimension; the spread of accounting ideas from country to country,

ii) Universal Accounting: this includes attempts at harmonization, at achieving similar levels of disclosure and similar methods of measurement from one country to another,

iii) Comparative accounting: one reason for describing and comparing the different accounting practices that exist around the world is to enable the accountant to understand the differences and so be able to assess their effects on financial reports. Weirich Avely and Anderson (1971) referred to 'The International Accounting System',

iv) the technical problems of parent-foreign subsidiary accounting, foreign currency translation, segmented accounts, and primary and secondary statements.

Fantle (1968) refers to three major concepts in international accounting: one, a universal system; two, a descriptive and informative approach covering all the methods and standards of all countries; and three, accounting practices of foreign subsidiaries and parent companies. Weirich, et al (1971) in surveying the literature at that time on the subject, used similar classifications. Jennings (1962) sees it as that set of accounting and auditing standards which could be accepted internationally. He would define it as universal or world accounting (similar to (ii) above). Jennings hoped that research programmes would provide the beginning of the development of international standards of accounting and auditing. He saw international conferences as being an important step in the process of standardising accounting and auditing practices. Zimmerman (1971), who with his colleagues at the University of Illinois has done as much as anyone to increase academic involvement in the international aspects of the subject, believed that "international accounting could be considered as an abstraction of the highest order of accounting"; he hoped that the subject would develop universal theories that would not be limited to any national boundaries, but would be applicable to accounting in any country.

Some writers (Kollaritsch (1965), Mueller (1967) and Mahon (1965)) see it as the study and analysis of the variety of principles, methods and standards of accounting of all countries (similar to (iii) above). They refer to this as international accounting and some writers (e.g. Bowles (1968)) see the subject as being primarily concerned with the accounting problems and practices of multinational operations of accounting for foreign subsidiaries (included in (iv) above).

Weirich et al (1971) distinguished between world accounting, which they see as a universal system that could be adopted in all countries and international accounting which includes one set of accounting standards for all countries, together with a different possible set of accounting standards for a particular country. The result would be, for companies in some countries, two sets of accounts being prepared. They recognise that no universal or perfect set of principles could be expected to be established. This is because of different geographic, socio-economic, political and legal influences. Mueller (1970) makes a similar point in a paper which is concerned with the research on multinational accounting problems.

The AAA's International Committee (1981) classify the research in international accounting up to that time as being in three main areas: one, the descriptive and comparative; two, "establishing international accounting standards", and three, analysing the particular accounting problems which confront multinational corporations. These three categories conform to three of those listed above. Reference is also made by the Committee to work on international auditing standards and to the work on accounting education in different countries, but these are seen as being separate topics.

Berg, Mueller and Walker (1969) see international accounting as being concerned with (i) the "international implications of the various national accounting thoughts and practices and (ii) measures and communications, in financial and economic terms, of international business events and transaction". This is a very wide definition and certainly embraces all the different aspects of the subject referred to above.

It is not always easy to categorise an article or an author's definition on international accounting under one of these subsets. Mueller (1965), states "International accounting is concerned with inter-relationships of accounting amongst countries". This would seem a sufficiently wide definition to embrace all the concepts referred to above, indeed, wide enough to embrace the fourth aspect, the historical dimension.

An interesting research study that indicates the range and number of problems in international accounting was that by Scott and Troberg (1980) entitled "88 International Accounting Problems: in rank order of importance". The authors adopted the Delphi technique to rank the different problems in order of perceived importance. The technique involves seeking the opinions of experts in the field, and in the final phase of the study, 41 such international accounting experts participated.

International accounting problems were divided by the authors into nine categories and the research resulted in these being ranked in order of importance. The first, the most important problem, was seen to be exchange rate and currency translation accounting problems. The second most important was international accounting education, and then followed, in order, international accounting standards; international auditing problems; accounting disclosures; accounting for inflation in international operations; international information and control systems problems. The least important being seen as international tax accounting.

These categories are, with one exception, a mixture of problems relating to harmonisation, and the technical problems of parent-foreign subsidiary accounting. The exception is that of international accounting education, the problem of a lack of adequately trained accountants in many countries.

It is clearly difficult to define international accounting; from the above definitions and the perceived problems it can be seen that the topics it embraces are wide. It would seem that there are international aspects of all branches of accounting. For convenience, the subject of accounting is usually divided into a number of subsets, a number of branches. Enthoven (1970 and 1981), refers to these as macro accounting, embracing national accounting, (sometimes referred to as social or economic accounting) and micro accounting which includes business (or enterprise) accounting and government accounting. Each branch can be further divided between a control element (including auditing) and a reporting element. It can be argued that each of these branches and subsets has a domestic and international element. The position can be illustrated as below:

	Domestic	International
Macro		
National		
Control	x	x
Reporting	x	x
Micro		
Government		
Control	x	x
Reporting	x	x
Enterprise		
Control	x	x
Reporting	x	x

International Accounting is not therefore so much a branch of accounting as a strata, a cross section of accounting. There are international aspects of all branches of accounting. Any syllabus in the subject, therefore, that wishes to be comprehensive must be very wide. Any survey article must also cover a wide area. It is true that some aspects of international accounting have attracted much more attention than others.

c) Outline of the Survey

The survey will not attempt to cite all the papers that have been written in the field of international accounting. The subject is far too wide to be able to do that. Bibliographies on the subject have already been published, (Kubin and Mueller 1973, Gray 1974, Mason 1978, Houghton 1979, Agami and Kollaritsch 1983). The Accounting Review has issued a bibliography on articles that it has published over the period from 1926 to 1978 and this contains a section on international accounting. The International Journal of Accounting has issued an index of articles it has published from 1966 to 1981.

In addition to these bibliographies, there are a number of textbooks on international accounting and accounting for multinational companies. These include Mueller (1967) Enthoven (1970), Scot (1970) Watt, Hammer and Burge (1977), Choi and Mueller(1978 and 1984) and Nobes and Parker (1981). Further textbooks on accounting for multinational business are mentioned in Chapter 5. Each of these textbooks provide bibliographies on the various issues they cover. In addition to textbooks there are books of readings. (Berg, Mueller and Walker 1969, American Accounting Association 1979, Choi and Mueller 1979). There are also numerous reports on international accounting; for example, those of the American Accounting Association (1973) (1976) (1977) (1978) and suggested programmes for future research, (Mueller 1979, Choi 1981, American Accounting Association 1981).

International accounting covers a wide area, at least as wide as national accounting. As can be seen from the above two paragraphs, the literature on the subject has already been well digested. This survey will attempt to be comprehensive, in that it will mention all aspects of international accounting, but it will not be possible to provide an even coverage of all aspects, certain sub-areas will be examined in more detail than others. The areas chosen for more detailed consideration are those which are particularly important or where the existing literature is confusing or inadequate.

In a survey article the author has the choice of three approaches to the subject; (1) a statement on the 'state of the art' at a particular point of time with the author's personal comments on the current position; (2) an historical development of the subject; and (3) a rapid run through of the books and articles on the subject. There is a danger that a survey article can fall between these three roles. This survey can perhaps be criticised in that it contains an element of all these three roles. For example, Chapter 2 is an historical development, the chapter on harmonization is largely a state of the art, and the chapter on international dimensions of accounting and financial reporting practices is a rapid run through of some of the literature on the subject.

This survey looks at international accounting in its wide perspective, because it is felt to do otherwise can give a misleading impression. There is more to international accounting than for example, multinational reporting and classifying countries into groups. Therefore there is a need for comprehensive coverage of the literature.

It would be possible to divide the chapters on the basis of the different branches of accounting referred to earlier, and to have, for example, one chapter on the international aspects of national income accounts, and another chapter on the international aspects of auditing and control in private sector business. This approach has, however, not been followed as the literature is unevenly divided between the branches of accounting. The material is divided into chapters on the basis of the areas of interest as reflected in the literature.

Following this introduction, Chapter 2 considers the way in which accounting ideas have spread over time from one country to another. This leads to Chapter 3, which covers the literature that describes, compares and contrasts the different accounting systems and practices that now exist in the countries of the world. In Chapter 4, the literature on the subject of harmonization and standardisation is analysed. Chapter 5 looks at international dimensions of accounting and financial reporting practices. Chapter 6 covers accounting and economic development, and Chapter 7 contains the conclusions.

Chapter Two

THE SPREAD OF IDEAS

a) Introduction

Anyone wishing to study and research International Accounting today who ignores how we have arrived at such a rich variety of accounting practices is making a serious error. To write about harmonising accounting practices, for example, without considering why different approaches have been adopted in different countries can be seen as a mistake.

There are many excellent books of readings on the history of accounting and in particular on the development of accounting thought. Amongst these are Brown (1905), Littleton and Yamey (1956), Garner and Hughes (1978) and Lee and Parker (1979). A number of these books are issued in the Arno Press series on "The Development of Contemporary Accounting Thought". A recent relevant publication is a guide to "Historical Accounting Literature" edited by Bywater and Yamey (1982).

The literature indicates that the spread of ideas between countries occurs either because:

a) a new idea is so technically far ahead of existing methods, that resistance to change is overcome and the new idea adopted.

b) a foreign power so dominates politically or through trade the host country, that the techniques of the foreign power are adapted even though they may be more suited to a different social and political background.

c) a large amount of capital has moved from one country, the home country, to be invested in another country, the host-country, and accounting methods move with it.

d) one country has no organised body of accounting principles, and is willing to adopt existing ideas from other countries.

Nobes and Parker (1981) link the spread of accounting ideas to a) trade, b) empires, or at least the influence of economically powerful nations, c) the spread of multinational businesses, multinational banks and accounting firms, d) international agencies, e) international conferences and meetings of professional accountants and f) education and research.

Perhaps the most oft quoted reason now being given for the study of international accounting, is that business is becoming increasingly more international, and so a more uniform approach to accounting policies and practice would make sense. If some degree of harmonization could be achieved it is said it would further encourage the movement of capital between countries and would further encourage international trade. This argument has an intuitive appeal.

It is true that there are now large multinational companies who are responsible for much of the movement of capital between one country and another, and who through their intra-company trading are often responsible for much of a country's foreign trade. But there is nothing new about capital moving from one country to another, or about international trade. Most of the countries of the world have financed their development from foreign borrowing and until recent years most of this was private lending and borrowing (Sampson 1981). The USA was in 1914 the largest debtor in the world. The UK had helped finance its development by borrowing from Central European Bankers. It was usually portfolio investment rather than the direct investment of the modern multinational company, but it can be argued the scale was as great. In relative terms, therefore, has international trade and investment become more important?

The UK's overseas investments in the 19th century as a proportion of its GNP was greater than the USA's overseas investments to GNP in the 1970s. Between 1875 and 1914, there were years when more than half of the savings in the UK were invested in foreign assets. With regard to trade, the UK in the 19th century was more dependent on trade than the USA is today. The Venetians in the 15th century were probably more dependent on trade than 19th century UK. The Egyptians 3000 years ago were big traders, as were the Hindus 5000 years ago. The argument that if we want to encourage international investment and trade we need high standards of disclosure and a harmonized system of accounting does not seem to stand up in an historical context. Why did the UK invest in the USA in the 19th century when at that time the USA hardly had an accounting profession? The answer is that if the possible returns are large enough, the risk (the uncertainties in this context) are worthwhile. Investment is a matter of balancing returns against the level of risk. The South Sea bubble showed investors taking large risks, they had very little knowledge about where they were investing, but they were prepared to take the risk (in this case they lost).

The argument for harmonized accounting across countries is an argument for reducing the risks associated with international investment. This is a reasonable argument, but the evidence indicates that international investment will take place on a large scale even if accounting harmonization cannot be achieved. It could be that increased disclosure and a greater understanding could lead to more worries and anxieties and so reduce the level of investment.

The point being made is that international accounting should not be seen as something new that has come about because of the recent growth of multinational business operations. There has always been international trade and investment and there has always been international accounting. The earliest traders and international investors were just as interested in the international aspects of accounting as we are now. They were interested in foreign currency conversion and translation. They looked at different approaches in different countries, and the best ideas spread from one country to another. The same process is at work today (Bedford 1966). Just as today the multinational businessmen and the firms of international accountants are trying to spread around the world what they believe are the best accounting practices, so the Hindu traders spread their ideas and much later the Italian City States helped spread double entry ideas. These points will be illustrated later in this chapter.

One reason why the interest in international accounting has grown is that there has been a significant growth over the last 20 years in the multinational operation of the large accounting firms. The profession has become increasingly aware and interested in the problems of their own and their clients multinational operations. According to a Fortune survey, in 1977 of the total reported revenues of the big accounting firms practising in the USA, 39% came from foreign operations. The importance of foreign operations varied firm by firm, with Price Waterhouse at 49% showing the highest foreign dependence (Buckley and O'Sullivan 1980). Wu and Hackett (1977), have shown that the number of foreign offices of US firms exceeds domestic offices by a ratio of 2 to 1. To the multinational accounting firms, all aspects of international accounting are obviously of importance.

As Bedford (1966) explains "historically the process by which accounting procedures and thought have been transmitted from one country to another has been by the physical transfer of accountants". In ancient times accounting ideas spread in the same way, but movement was slower and there was not so much of it. The spread and amount of movement of accountants and business has accelerated. For a collection of readings on the evolution of accounting thought see Chatfield (1968).

The importance of the spread of ideas is not always recognised. Many accountants practising within a particular country do not aways appreciate that what they see as say, UK accounting practice or US accounting practice has in fact been imported from another country. One of the earlist writers to recognise the importance of the spread of ideas was Henry Hatfield. He was a pioneer in accounting education at universities in the United States (see Mumford 1980) and in 1911 he addressed the Annual Convention of the American Association of Public Accountants. The paper was entitled 'Some Variations in Accounting Practice in England, France, Germany and the United States'. The paper was not in fact, published until 1966, over fifty years later. He pointed out to his audience that, "It is to be recognised that foreign and American accounting methods are at heart one. Accounting in all the modern world has developed from the same simple beginnings". Much of the paper consists of a comparison of accounting practices in the different countries. It will be referred to again in the comparative section of this book. He points out to his audience that the US had tended to look to England rather than the Continent for accounting inspirations. "Our system of certifying Public Accounts is based on English models and the examination questions are frequently cribbed from those set in London". He goes on to say that the standard of bookkeeping among commercial people is far higher on the continent of Europe than in the United Kingdom. "Continental bookkeeping is more methodical, more cumbrous, more tenacious of inherited forms than British and much more so than American". He introduces his audience to the advanced works on accounting published in Germany and France.

Zeff (1972) has shown examples of the transfer of accounting ideas on an international basis. He makes reference to the Scottish Institute drawing unofficially on the recommendations of the English Institute and to the Mexican profession paying considerable attention to the Bulletins of the US Institute. With reference to Canada he comments on the influence of the USA taking over from the traditional reliance on the UK.

Zeff, when writing about the transference of ideas and practices from one country to another, comments that it would be intriguing to study this transference. To study the process, to see how it works. He refers to an article by Enthoven (1969), describing that article as perhaps the best recent example of transference through cross-pollination of literature. The Enthoven article having been reprinted in many languages.

In the remainder of this chapter an attempt is made to illustrate the spread of certain accounting ideas. This is bound to be inadequate for to do the job properly would result in a book with a number of volumes. Yamey (1981) points to the problem of trying to piece together the history of accounting. He quotes Karl Peter Kheil, a Bohemian banker and scholar, who attempted for forty years to write the history of bookkeeping and accounting, who shortly before his death concluded, "One has to be content with fragments of all contributions to the history of bookkeeping, so long as the sources and the collected manuscripts and printed materials necessary for a general history of the science had not been fully researched, winnowed and tested". (Quoted in Penndorf 1913). Yamey makes the point that in writing a history of accounting, one should not confine oneself to Europe and North America.

b) Ancient Accounting

Sombart saw double-entry bookkeeping as a major influence on economic development. "One can scarcely conceive of capitalism without double entry bookkeeping, they are related in form and content." He believed double entry released, activated and stimulated the rationalisatic pusuit of profits on capital. His writings have led to much debate.

Yamey (1964) supports Sombart's thesis that "the system of double entry bookkeeping was an active catalyst in the economic expansion that occurred in Europe following the close of the Middle Ages". Winjum (1971) agrees "double entry's capacity to accumulate data on individual operative activities, combined with its ability to bring order to affairs of (the merchants) stimulated and rationalised the economic activities of the early English merchants".

Capitalism may have needed accounting, but accounting did not need capitalism. A number of writers have disagreed with Sombart's thesis. (For a discussion see Previts 1975). Most (1972) points out that "Accounting was not the product of the period of early capitalism but in fact was introduced into the public sector much earlier in time for planning and control purposes". Recently business enterprise accounting has become regarded as the leading aspect of accounting development but it has not always been so.

The history of accounting is more than the history of double-entry bookkeeping. The need to keep records of financial and other transactions is an ancient one. Systems of accounting information, modest as they were, can be traced back to early civilisations such as those of Mesopotamia, Egypt and Central America. As Littleton (1933) pointed out when discussing what had been written about the history of accounting "And when it is all put together what do they have but a surmise as to how it all came about?"

It is true we do not know a great deal about the history of the subject, but there does seem some evidence that it existed in India many thousands of years ago. As long ago as 1798 Hamilton wrote "we would remark that the Banians of India have been, from time immemorial, in possession of the method of bookkeeping by double entry, and that Venice was the emporium of Indian commerce at the time at which Friar Lucas's (Paciolis') treatise appeared". Unfortunately as Yamey (1956) points out Hamilton did not indicate the basis for his remarks.

Sodhbans, a UK qualified accountant practising in India, presented a paper at the International

Congress of Accountants in Berlin in September 1938. The 1938 conference was held in a very nationalistic environment. Sodhbans described the development of the Hindu Empire 7,000 to 8,000 years BC. At that time there was extensive overseas trade with colonial possessions and this necessitated a serviceable system of bookkeeping and accounting. He claims bookkeeping had its origin in that part of the world in those early days:

> With such high standards of civilisation and with mastery over international trade and commerce, the Indians of that period could not carry on trade without a proper system of accounting and therefore it is but a natural conclusion that the double entry system of accounting was invented originally by the Indians and was borrowed from India by Arabs, Egyptians, Phoenicians or Italians who had trade connections with India.

What of the evidence? Sodhbans mentions that "The Periplus of the Erythreean sea" leaves no doubt that commerce and trade reached such a magnitude that it could not be carried on without a proper record of accounting. (See also Choudhury 1982). Certainly there is evidence that a revenue and financial system of government accounting evolved under Emperor Akbar. Indeed it is claimed by Sodhbans that the same old system which is called "Bahi-Khata" is still being used by the Indian Merchants in an undiluted form.

Webster (1937) states "all or most of the few books on the history of accounting have begun with Assyria and Egypt, leaped over many centuries to Italy". Many writers make reference to the beginnings being in the Middle East. Keister (1965) describes the scribe of Mesopotamia as the predecessor of todays accountant, and in an introduction to a reprint of this article, Chatfield (1969) makes the point that "the record keeping, verification and internal control problems encountered by ancient societies were in many ways similar to our own". It seems likely that the ideas spread to the Middle East from India as a result of the trade between the regions. The Egyptian Pharoahs did have a form of internal financial control operating within their Treasury in about 3,000 BC. European civilisation began to emerge around, 2,800 BC in Crete. The Cretans had elementary knowledge of accounting, with most of the records being concerned with tax assessment and with inventory records. The knowledge, not surprisingly, moved to nearby Greece.

There has been a great deal of interest shown by historians and accounting historians in the accounting techniques of ancient Greece and Rome. The point at issue being the level of sophistication of the accounting techniques employed. De ste. Croix (1956) in one of the leading articles on the subject concludes that the bookkeeping "minutely detailed as it often was, remained rudimentary in method" and took the form of "individual records of debts and of receipts and payments". (See also Costouros, 1979). Because of problems with numerical notation, it has been pointed out how difficult it was to keep what are now regarded as proper books of accounts. Many years later When the Arabs introduced Hindu Arabic numerals into Europe that it became possible to make significant improvement in accounting records (see De ste. Croix 1956).

When the Empire of the Greeks declined, the Roman Empire developed and it benefitted from the infusion of the Greek administrative tradition. The system evolved slowly. Again taxation was the main reason for keeping records. There were, however, laws introduced to ensure that money lenders retained accounting records. Braudel (1973) points out that Rome was familiar with current accounts and debits and credits in moneylenders' books. Concepts such as depreciation were familiar to the Greeks and Romans, where for example walls were depreciated at an annual rate of one eightieth of the cost.

When the Roman Empire collapsed, the accounting techniques that had evolved did not disappear; they moved in two directions; one movement was through the early Christian Church that had capable administrators and had built up substantial estates. Many of these estates were outside Italy and spread as far as Southern Gaul. The religious orders kept accounting records of their household estates.

There is evidence that many years later, Kings of the Francs, for example, Charlemagne, employed ecclesiastical advisors who kept records of their estates. (See De Roover 1956). Similar procedures had been adopted by the Kings of England. King Alfred, 871-901 reorganised the national finances and by the year 1012, a system of national taxation had been instituted. This required the keeping of accounting records. The Normans had developed a system of centralised financial administration and they introduced this into England after the Conquest. The spread of ideas at the time was concerned with governmental accounting.

Reference was made to accounting records following two paths out of Rome; one was the Christian Church; the other was a movement to the East, to Constantinople. This was part of the Byzantine Empire. Runciman (1961) believes that, "The administrative machinery of the Byzantine was expensive and cumbersome, but it was sufficiently elastic and so long as the Empire's finances remained sound, extremely efficient". "To the end the administration retained an efficiency unknown in Western Europe".

In the eleventh and twelfth century there then came about a combining of knowledge, a fusion of the Eastern and Western approaches. The Crusaders invaded the Middle East. The Byzantine Empire began to collapse. The city states of Northern Italy freed themselves from the control of the German Empire and began to take over the trade of the Byzantine Empire. Venice benefitted from the Crusades and a new Empire was formed with Venice dominating the trade in the Near East. It was at the time the Crusaders opened up the trade in the Near East to the Italians and the latter began an acquaintance with the achievements of the Byzantine and Arab civilisations that double-entry accounting appeared in Italy.

In the fifth to the thirteenth centuries Europe was a backwater. It was the Byzantine and Arabic cultures that dominated. No other states could compete with the wealth of medieval Islam and the Byzantine. It was the money that was the instrument of power (Braudel 1973). In fact there were not only Muslims engaged in business but also Jews and Christians. In the ninth to the eleventh centuries there were partnerships between Jewish Merchants of distant lands (Ben Sassoon 1976). From the tenth and eleventh centuries the Italian money changers began to grow in importance and to assume a position of dominance in the financial affairs of Western and Central Europe. It was out of this environment, this meeting together of ideas that double-entry bookkeeping emerged.

The first publication of a formal treatise on accounting is usually said to be that of Pacioli in 1494. This was indeed one of the first books printed on any topic. There is, however, evidence that double-entry bookkeeping was operational long before this book was published (Brown 1905). As

Raymond de Roover (1956) writes, the origin is "complicated and confused". The system evolved rather than was the result of 'the genius of the individual'. "Double entry did not grow out of any pre-established theory but was developed step by step by a process of trial and error".

There is a large amount of literature on the origin of double-entry bookkeeping. For details of the rival claims, see Brown (1905), Yamey (1956), de Roover (1956), Croix (1956), Parker (1971), Lee (1973) and Bailey (1983). Littleton (1933) lists the ingredients, the elements, that he believes were necessary before double-entry bookkeeping could be developed. He sees such elements as essential to the formation of double entry, necessary but not sufficient conditions. These elements were all present in ancient civilization, but did not lead to double entry being developed. It was the changes in outlook and surroundings, in mens aspirations and interests, and in the differences in the quantity of wants and quality of ideas that led to double entry emerging in the Middle Ages rather than in earlier periods.

The weight of evidence indicates that it developed in Italy. Knowledge of the technique spread slowly through the rest of Europe. de Roover (1956) speaks highly of the advanced state of Flemish bookkeeping in the fourteenth century and claims this was due to the Italian influence. He claims that the fourteenth and fifteenth centuries was perhaps the most brilliant and progressive period in the history of accounting. It was followed by a long period of stagnation that lasted until the nineteenth century. "The spread of double entry bookkeeping from Italy to the rest of Europe and thence further afield was largely the result of the influence of treatise describing and exaplaining the system and its practice and of business practices in Italy and those of Italian merchants elsewhere which were copied by others whom came into contact with them". Local influences would however result in slight variations in the practice of bookkeeping. Double-entry bookkeeping spread slowly through Europe. Ympyn (1547) describes the direction of the flow, when introducing the English language edition of his book - he explains that it was translated out of Italian into Dutch, out of Dutch into French, and out of French into English. By the 16th century commercial supremacy had moved out of Italy to Flanders and the Netherlands. Simon Stevin of Bruges writing in 1602 made a significant contribution to the subject, when he introduced what is now known as the present value concept. (See Ten Have 1956).

The later contribution of some other countries will now be considered.

c) The UK/US Contribution

Yamey (1977) details the slow adoption of double entry bookkeeping in England between 1500 and 1900. It was the development of the accounting profession that was a major influence in its adoption. Yamey raises a point which is as relevant to the spread of ideas today as it was to the period he was considering. "To what extent did the practice of accounting in the period depend upon forces operating from outside?" (i.e. coming from outside the enterprises and their particular requirements). "Might not attitudes towards say, double-entry bookkeeping in some cases, partly have reflected general cultural attitude".

One of the major contributions of the UK to accounting was the development of professional bodies. This began in Scotland, when a group of accountants obtained recognition for their body. A Society of Accountants in Edinburgh obtained a Royal Charter in 1854. The English Institute obtained theirs in 1880. The idea of professional bodies for accountants soon spread to other countries.

Late in the 19th century and early in the 20th century, UK accounting firms started establishing offices in other countries. Deloitte, Deve, Griffiths and Co., opened offices in 17 foreign cities between 1890 and 1914 (Kettle 1958). By the middle of the 19th century there were still very few people practising accounting in the USA (in 1850, only 19 accountants names were listed in the City Directories of New York, Chicago and Philadelphia). (Littleton 1942, Previts and Merino 1979). By the 1880's the number of persons offering their services as accountants had considerably increased. A number of these had come from and been trained in Britain. This movement of skilled people was accompanying the movement of capital.

The Institute of Accountants and Bookkeepers formed in New York in 1882 was the first professional accounting organisation in the USA. At a meeting in 1886 a member presented a paper to the Institute entitled "French and American Account-Keeping Contrasted" - a similar topic to many papers to appear over the next 100 years! Previts refers to this as "the first known professional address on international accounting matters in America" (USA).

British auditors had begun to live in the USA as English firms began to set up resident offices in US cities. This British contingent served as a nucleus influencing the founding of the American Association of Public Accountants (AAPA) in 1887. The first president of the Association being an Englishman. As well as the two bodies mentioned a number of other US professional accounting bodies were being formed across the country.

Early professional activities were marked by the existence of these two camps, the British and the Americans. This is similar to patterns that have emerged in developing countries in recent years with a body representing nationally qualified accountants competing with those with a foreign qualification. The two main rival organisations in the US at the end of the 19th century were the AAPA and the New York based Institute of Accountants and Bookkeepers. Both bodies were preparing bills hoping to have these passed by the State of New York.

The St. Louis Conference of 1904 was an attempt to bring some sort of agreement and some uniformity amongst the many powerful societies that developed across the US. A number of practitioners met in 1902 to discuss means of forming a national group to promote CPA laws in every state. The fruit of their efforts was the organisation of the Federation of Societies of Public Accountants. The Federation's announced goal was to seek CPA legislation in most States. The St. Louis meeting was "a milestone in the development of accountancy in the United States " (Previts and Merino 1979). The most difficult task facing the delegates at the 1902 meeting and the 1904 Congress was to convince practitioners that their professional interest could be best promoted by a national organisation. Subsequent to the negotiations at the congress the Federation agreed to merge with the AAPA. Although many participating at the conference viewed the merger of the two national organisations as the first step in obtaining a united profession it soon became apparent that the new body that was formed did not have the authority to force meaningful professional standards. The St. Louis conference was an attempt to unite accountants of the United States. The International element is, one can suggest, merely window dressing designed to increase the status of the profession within the USA, to persuade non-accountants in the US of the importance and significant of the US bodies (Samuels 1985).

Johnson and Caygill (1971) illustrate how the various British professional accounting bodies have exerted influence on accounting in many other countries of the world. They show how this influence has been achieved by the movement of accountants from the UK, the spread of overseas branches of the British bodies, by many people from the Commonwealth taking British qualifications, and by the assistance provided in the creation of local accounting bodies.

Initially local associations of accountants were established by migrants from Britain (as in the case of the USA). They often followed "in the wake of British capital and commerce". Not dissimilar to the way in which ideas of international accounting standards are now following in the new wave of multinational capital and commerce. Generally speaking, local associations of accountants are first established by migrants from Britain, many of them having been members of British accountancy bodies. The Accountant published in London was using, well into this century, the sub title "The Recognised Weekly Organ of Chartered Accountants and Accountancy Throughout the World".

In 1956 the President of the English Institute commented, "Anyone who examines the history of the profession in almost any country of the world, cannot fail to be impressed by the major part played by Chartered Accountants from the United Kingdom in the world development of the profession". (The Accountant 1956).

Problems arose in the British Commonwealth over the use of the term chartered, and the English Institute took the line that the granting of a Charter by the Sovereign was the only way in which any body could use the expression Chartered Accountant. In 1926 the South African accountants who were introducing a bill into the South African Parliament wished to use the title Chartered Accountants of South Africa. Many South Africans did not see why on grounds of equity or justice, accountants practising in South Africa who had qualified in England, Ireland, Scotland, Wales or Canada should be permitted to use the title Chartered Accountants while South African trained accountants should be denied the priviledge in their own country of this title. It was pointed out that the future of the profession in South Africa must lie with the locally trained younger man. By 1926 very few of the people coming into accounting in South Africa were immigrants from overseas chartered societies. (The Accountant, December 11th, 1926).

This is a similar argument to that which has been used in many countries of Africa and Asia in the 1960s and 1970s. Local Associations of Accountants have been formed and these have needed to compete for prestige with foreign trained accountants. This aspect of international accounting will be returned to in the section dealing with accounting and economic development.

In addition to the introduction of an accounting profession the US and UK have made many other major contributions to the development of accounting. These include, the UK being responsible for the early progress of auditing as a subject, and the US development in management accounting and consolidated accounts. These ideas quickly spread from one country to another. The early development of auditing in the UK is discussed by Edey and Panitpakdi (1956) and Lee (1979). Dicksee's auditing was the first major work on the subject (1st edition 1892). It was described in its subtitle as "a practical manual for auditors". Dicksee placed emphasis on identifying, elaborating and explaining the methods to be adopted by auditors. The book was a success both in the USA and UK. The first 'Authorised American Edition' was published in 1905, being edited by Robert H. Montgomery. It has been said that Montgomery's adoption of Dicksee's text to American needs in 1905 marked the beginning of American literature in Accounting (Kitchen 1981). A second American Edition was published in 1909.

Lee (1979) writing on the evolution of accounting in the UK, quotes from the work of Hein, dealing with the period 1844-1962. Hein demonstrates that there was an understandable reluctance in both the UK and USA to be regulated by legislation. There was even at one time an unwillingness in the UK to self-regulate. In the US, public regulation has become accepted. In the UK the accounting profession tries to limit the extent of statutory control preferring to rely on self-regulation and court decisions. Certain countries have followed the approach of Britain, others that of the USA. (See Benston 1976).

The professional accounting press are

instrumental in spreading ideas. The Accountant of 5th September 1903, makes the point that although accounting is a new profession in the United States there are certain aspects of accounting in that country that could be usefully copied by people in the UK. United States manufacturers, it is said, have shown themselves quick to appreciate the advantages of having a respected accounting profession. The manufacturers are willing to listen to accountants, they are willing to listen to any ideas that help reduce costs. The article is critical of "the notorious conservatism of British manufacturers". The point being made is that UK manufacturers do not listen to accountants and are not quick to appreciate ideas that will save them money. There is another criticism in the article, this one directed at the profession in the UK. The point is made that few accountants are interested in cost accounting although there is considerable scope for the development of the subject in the UK. Cost accounting as a subject was at the time more or less ignored in professional examinations.

Reference is also made to early American creativity in accounting. It is pointed out that at the turn of the century there was much abuse in financial reporting in the USA. There is however much to admire in particular "an exhibition of American adaptability and inventiveness. So successful have American accountants been in devising forms suited to the desired ends, that on the continent, any bookkeeping device that is recognised as having peculiar merit and originality is, irrespective of its actual origin, apt to be called American Bookkeeping".

The US were the first country to develop holding company accounts. A. L. Dickenson (later Sir Arthur) delivered a lecture at the 1904 St. Louis Congress in which he spoke of the advantage of showing the profits and losses of the whole group of companies. He was at the time head of the New York office of Price Waterhouse. Later he moved to the London office and gave a lecture to the Royal Statistical Society in 1924 in which he made reference to accounting practices in the United States in comparison with Great Britain. He said "In the United States the almost universal practice for more than 15 years past has been for holding company groups to publish a consolidated statement of the earnings and a consolidated balance sheet of all subsidiary companies. The practice in Great Britain is in its infancy and only a few concerns have yet adopted it". He made a further comment on accounting in the two countries when he said "Generally the practice in both countries has been in the past and appears to be still more so in the present to reduce rather than to increase the very inadequate information which is given with regard to earnings and cost". This is an example of the best practices of one country slowly being adopted in other countries. It was in fact not until 1947 that holding company accounts were required in the UK. The reasons for the delay have been discussed by Kitchin (1972), Walker (1976), Parker (1977), Lock (1978) and Mumford (1981).

d) The Continental European Contribution

Apart from the early Italian writers on double entry there have been many other Continental Europeans who have made major contributions to the subject as we know it today. Henry Hatfield (1924) in his historical defence of bookkeeping lists a number of important writers on the subject. These include Screiber (1518) from Germany, Stevin (1602) from the Netherlands and Savary (1675) from France.

This European tradition of accounting thought continued into the 20th century. Presenting a paper at the 1938 International Congress, Schybergson, a Finnish Professor, was able to say that "In comparison with the liveliness with which balance sheet problems are discussed in Germany, American literature on the subject strikes one as being rather dogmatic. The reason for this is to some extent the typical American practical mentality which has no time for abstract definitions or abstract ideas". The author goes on to explain that one reason why he thought this had come about, was that in the US the official supervision of public utilities brought into existence a carefully prescribed form of cost accounting. The author showed that certain cost ideas differed between Europe and the USA. He makes reference to the work on the economics of overhead costs, which is little known in Europe. This he regards as unfortunate, as it is claimed that as early as 1919 Schmalenbach had demonstrated that American practice and German theories of accounting were developing on parallel lines. The Americans reached their conclusion inductively by reasoning from the particular to the general and the Germans reached their's deductively by reasoning from the general to the particular.

Filios (1981) states that "during the first half of this century, accounting as a science seems to have been advanced in German and French speaking countries rather than in the English speaking world". In Germany the business economic school developed around the turn of the century and in 1906 a Journal on the subject was launched, edited by Schmalenbach, the founder of the school. Two years later he produced his first ideas on dynamic accounting. The German school and its variations within Germany had branches and followers in Holland, Switzerland and elsewhere in continental Europe. In particular it had great influence in France and Italy. Its ultimate purpose can be described as the analytical study of mainly private economic entities with a methodology that encompasses an integrated examination of their organisational administrative and economic and accounting aspects.

Schranz presented a paper at the 1938 Congress where he stated the German branch of business economics "is the most logical, systematic and architecturally perfect in the world". "It is only in the German cultural sphere that accountancy and business administration appears as an independent and uniform science". The writer may have been carried away a little by the nationalism that surrounded the 1938 Berlin Congress, but Germany does appear to have led in the development of a scientific approach to accounting.

At the same time that the German school was developing, in French-speaking Europe (France, Belgium and Switzerland) a parallel evolution was taking place. The first stage of this can be traced back to the theories of Cerboni (1873), whose work found wide acceptance in Italy as governmental accounting. A French writer in 1888, Barrachin, also developed a school of accounting. Schar (1922), who taught in Switzerland during the first years of the century and later in Berlin initiated the legalistic theories of accounting. The founder of the French school of economic accounting is considered to be Delaporte (1936), with Dumarchey (1914) as its leading theorist.

The German views on replacement cost accounting began to receive attention in the United States in the 1920s. The Accounting Review in September 1929 contained an article by Rorem. He argued that replacement cost should be the basic value for measuring business capital and income. Schmidt argued in a paper published in the USA in September

1930 that replacement cost offered the best basis for producing statements which would be useful both for current managerial control purposes and for use in planning mergers and reorganisation. He was concerned about the concept of profit. The profit of an undertaking, he stated, can only consist of what it produced above the maintenance of business assets.

The first article in the American literature on the effects of an unstable monetary unit on financial reports had been that by Middleditch in 1918. His article in the Journal of Accountancy appears to have had little effect. However, the period 1925-1935 was one in which American literature reflected an increasing interest in what was happening in Germany and France. (See Baily 1929) Articles by Sweeney and Wasserman (1931) reflect this interest.

Sweeney wrote articles (1927 and 1928) on the subject of German Inflation Accounting. His subsequent work on stabilised accounting owed a lot to the lessons he obtained from studying the German approach. Mumford (1979) makes reference to the fact that "Sweeney's book, Stabilized Accounting, published in 1936 linked American research and earlier European work of the 1920s and 1930s". Littleton was a big admirer of what was appearing in the German literature and he frequently reviewed German treatiseson the subject of inflation adjusted accounts. The 1930 volume of Accounting Review contains four articles by prominent German writers; in addition to Schmidt, there are articles by Schranz, Handorff and Volse.

At the Third International Congress held in New York in 1929, a paper on the valuation of assets had been presented by Schmidt. This was concerned with accounting at times of inflation. Schmidt's suggestion that "the work of German writers on the subject may be of help to our American bretheren" aroused little interest at the time. Forty years later writers in the UK and USA went over the same ground. Perhaps ideas do not spread as they should.

More recent German developments in price level accounting are reported by Coenenberg and Macharzina (1976). Their article traces the relationship between the work of Schmidt, Edwards and Bell and the recent German recommendations on inflation accounting. As well as the German and French influence on present ideas in inflation accounting there is also the important Dutch influence. Seven Sevanter (1969) considers the continuity postulate in the Dutch theory of business income. The writer compares the predominently pragmatic American accounting theory with the Dutch literature on accounting, which is characterised by a much greater emphasis on basic theory and general theoretical principles. The Dutch school, it is claimed, over the last fifty years, prove that a systematic body of accounting theory consistent with economics can be developed. Limperg was the leader of this school, which believed that the study of accounting should be integrated with the body of economic knowledge and methodology. (See Limperg's collected works 1964).

In fact in the USA at the end of the 19th century there had been some interest in replacement cost. It was a time of deflation and the government agencies tried to use replacement cost depreciation (with deflation, lower than historical cost depreciation) as a basis of calculating costs for setting railway charges. Current purchasing power ideas were also developed in the USA before the First World War by Irving Fisher (1911).

An article by Goudeket a Dutch academic, appeared in the Journal of Accountancy in July 1960, entitled "An application of replacement value theory". The editorial appearing in the Journal at the time of the article and subsequent letters to the Journal were very critical of this approach. The editorial referred to the procedures and described them as "Radical departures", a "revolution in accounting"; the editorial suggested that it was unlidely that accountants in the US would be interested in moving in the direction indicated. Here was an example of resistance to foreign ideas. Paton wrote a letter to the journal criticising the present position of the profession in the US. He felt that this rigid position had only come about during the 1940s and 1950s. He states, "how can a procedure which has been commonplace for years in leading industrial countries abroad be described as a radical departure?" He appreciated that it would be difficult to move the profession in the USA and suggested that, "it may well turn out that getting American accountants to mend their ways is as difficult as checking the Socialist trend here - a chore that looks almost impossible at the moment".

This provides an interesting comment on the spread of ideas, and the resistance to change in a receiving country. It lends some support to the comments made at the Berlin conference. It also shows how the position of countries can change in 20 years!

Interest in different aspects of accounting, in different ideas, rises and falls at different times. The USA was interested in 'National Uniform Charts of Accounts' in the 1910s and again in the 1930s, but then lost interest. The spread of ideas on uniform charts of accounts is considered by Karl Kafer (1965). The flow charts presented in the book by Schmalenbach were the basis of the systems adopted in many German industries. This book was published in 1927. There were further refinements to the charts in Germany in 1937 and 1949. Kafer compares these with the system, one of the first systems ever, which was the one founded in the USA and used by the American Waterworks Association in 1910. Kafer also contrasts the German system with the Austrian system and with the famous French system, the Plan Comptable of 1947 and 1957.

Kafer contrasts the US and European attitude towards charts of accounts. The point he makes is that the uniform accounting systems were never enforced upon industry in the US and UK as they had been in some countries of central Europe and Eastern Europe. There was never the same interest in the US and UK as elsewhere. The second point he makes is that the National European Standard System was designed to be applicable for all commercial and industrial enterprises. It was to be the basis for the 'charts of accounts' of major industries and these in turn were to be the basis for the charts of individual businesses. Kafer points out that it is part of a system designed to provide information for planning purposes.

Kafer draws attention to the fact that the subject of uniform accounts is now hardly ever mentioned in books and journals in the USA. This however was not always the case. "The early volumes of the Accountant's Index list hundreds of articles and pamphlets on the standard classification of accounts". He refers to a book written by Bently and Leonard published in 1935 which is a bibliography of works on accounting by American authors and this contains a supplement with a listing of publications on uniform accounting systems which takes up not less than 73 pages. The subject was discussed at the annual meetings of accounting bodies, the first of these mentioned being in 1913. Accountants in the USA were losing interest in the topic by the 1930s. An article critical of uniform accounts is that of Couchman (1934).

In Social Accounting the French and Germans have led the way. Both these countries require companies to disclose information to workers and consumers. (See Rey 1978, and Jaggi, 1980). Jaggi believes that the experience of German firms will have an impact on social accounting disclosures in other countries.

Many countries in addition to those mentioned above have made a contribution to the present state of knowledge in accounting. For example South American countries have been pioneers in introducing inflation accounting methods (see Baxter (1976), Zeff and Ovandoz (1975), Fleming (1974) and (1979), Scapens (1973)).

Doupnik (1982) describes and discusses Brazil's response to inflation, from its first attempts at indexation in the 1950s to the present time. He suggests that although at first other countries could learn from what was going on in Brazil, that now new inflation accounting developments in other countries means that Brazil could usefully study these alternative approaches (see also Baer and Beckerman 1980).

The above examples indicate that accounting is an international subject, that ideas spread from one country to another. There are interesting articles explaining how accounting ideas moved to particular countries, how they were adopted and adapted. The history of accounting in Russia is discussed by Bailey (1982); he points out that ideas spread to that country from Germany, UK, and Sweden, but that later Russia went on to develop its own system of accounting and "it should be remembered that Soviet Accounting has influenced accounting practice in countries as geographically separated as China, Czechoslavakia, and Cuba".

The adoption of accounting ideas in Japan is well discussed in the literature. In the February 27th, 1904 edition of The Accountant the Editorial draws readers attention to an advertisement which states that a certified or chartered accountant is required as a Professor of Accounting in a college in Japan. The point is made in the Editorial that Japan is well to the fore with an intelligent appreciation of the needs of the moment and that no doubt this appointment will bring considerable advantage to Japan.

In fact a proper bookkeeping method had been developed in Japan in 1700 and it continued in use in Japan until the beginning of the 1930s. (Ogura

1982, Fujita 1967, Nishikaw 1956). It was used by merchants of both large and medium size. The Western methods of accounting had been imported into Japan around 1870 and they were soon accepted and taught as an academic subject in commerical schools and in colleges but it was not immediately accepted or adopted for actual business practice in most Japanese business. The first actual users of the western system were the large industries that were being set up in the 1930s.

Japan came under the influence of the Western world a little over a century ago and until 1949 they fashioned many of their Institutions on German and other European models. Since the second world war, the influence of the United States has become noticeable and much stronger.

Accounting ideas are still spreading from country to country. The current attempts to harmonize accounting standards and practices can be seen as a part of this international movement of ideas. The spread of double entry ideas and inflation accounting techniques from country to country are just as much international accounting as for example the attempts to encourage all countries to adopt the same foreign currency translation techniques. On occassions writers in the international accounting area ignore history, they do not consider why a particular country has adopted a particular reporting practice. Sometimes the accounting system was imposed on a country without any particular thought as to whether it was the best system for that country. The accounting practices in a country are continually changing. The direction in which they move depends on internal economic changes within the country and upon outside influences. This leads to the interesting area of the international accounting literature in which different accounting systems are compared and contrasted. In which attempts are made to explain why a country has a particular system.

Chapter Three

DESCRIPTIVE, COMPARATIVE AND CLASSIFICATION

a) Introduction

A large amount of the literature on international accounting has been concerned with either describing the accounting methods of a particular country, or with comparing the methods of one country or a group of countries with those of another country or group of countries. For convenience these articles and books can be divided into three elements each covering a different method of research. The chapter follows the same breakdown. The first part covers the literature which can be called descriptive but which often does contain some element of comparison. Such literature describes all or some aspect of the accounting system in a country or a number of countries. Although in some of the work more than one country may be covered, the comparative aspect does not amount to classification. Sometimes it is a description of the accounting principles and practices in one of the large industrialised countries, sometimes a system in a less well known country, sometimes a description of an unusual aspect of one particular country's accounting methods.

A second element of the literature is concerned with comparative research which leads to classification of countries into groups but not classification based on statistical techniques. Such work is discursive comparative research based on observing different financial reporting patterns and drawing conclusions as to how these different patterns have developed. A third part of the literature uses statistical techniques to classify different countries accounting systems into groups. Usually the statistical technique used is factor analysis. Classification is an important aspect of international accounting in that it attempts to "sharpen description and analysis" (AAA 1977).

Descriptive, Comparative and Classification

Descriptive articles can be interesting and useful but if we wish to organise our knowledge of accounting around the world in order to make meaningful observations we need to classify. We know countries have different systems, we need to know why.

Goodrich (1981) in an interesting article entitled 'Competing Paradigms in Comparative International Accounting' attempts to compare and contrast the advantages and disadvantages of the different approaches to research in this area. The three classes of research mentioned above correspond to what Goodrich sees as "three competing paradigms", three basic approaches to theory development. Goodrich refers to the first of these above approaches as the case study basis, the second as the development of an overview of different national accounting system types, and the third as the factor analysis approach.

Paradigms help to interpret and analyse disparate facts. International accounting is full of disparate facts. Paradigms help problem solving by pinpointing the most important factors to be considered, and hopefully help remove some of the ambiguity in a problem. All these approaches to research, all three paradigms, have contributed something in helping to unravel the complexities of accounting around the world. It is not clear why we should see the alternative approaches as competing, why at conferences people should debate the merits of one approach as opposed to another. We should be trying to identify the good and bad points of each, and co-ordinating research using all three approaches. Goodrich believes that there is at present no single paradigm which dominates the field. There are indeed a number of approaches to research in addition to the three mentioned. "Thus comparative international accounting researches can benefit greatly by using relevant and appropriate portions of the competing paradigms". (Goodrich 1981)

b) Descriptive and comparative research (based on the case study approach)

This type of research, the country by country study, has three particular uses: (i) it can be extremely helpful to those in practice who do actually want to make comparisons of the accounts of a company in one country with those of a company in another country. The detailed work of researchers such as Beeny (1976), Beeny and Chastney (1978) and others make such comparisons easier. (ii) It has an educational value, making readers aware of the differences in the reporting methods country by country. There is a danger in that it is easy to think that the system with which one is most familiar is the best.

Seidler (1967) explains how it is possible to use examples taken from around the world to illustrate unresolved accounting problems in a particular country. This is linked to the spread of ideas, being the willingness to examine what has been tried in other countries to see if it has any relevance to the problem of another country. Seidler believes that the study of international accounting gives "the opportunity to bring practical experience to bear on what were formerly purely theoretical discussions". He quotes the work of Goudeket (1960) on the application of replacement value theory, Holzer and Schonfield (1963) on index linked depreciation and Garnier (1962) on uniform accounting systems as being particularly relevant. Since the date of Seidler's article there have of course been many more studies published that would be appropriate to the type of course he had in mind.
(iii) the third use of this form of research, a detailed analysis of the system in one country, is that it is a necessary beginning for research that attempts to classify.

Goodrich (1981) believes "the best way for comparative international accounting to proceed is to start at the bottom of the ladder of abstraction". Country by country studies can be seen as being at the lowest level of abstraction (Sartori 1973). Accounting researchers such as Ijiri (1972) believe that descriptive models in accounting should be as general as possible. We have not yet achieved this general approach, which is the highest level of abstraction. "One approach to advancing the field of international accounting is to attempt to start at the top and try immediately to produce a general model, another approach is to start at the bottom of the ladder of abstraction, with country by country studies and then attempt to move up through the middle range of abstraction to the general. In this ladder, the middle ranges are represented by intra-area studies, by comparative research perhaps using factor analysis"(Ijiri 1972). The point being made is that descriptive country by country analysis is one approach to research the subject of international accounting, but it is only a beginning.

An outstanding example of early good work in the field is that of Henry Hatfield. His 1911 paper describes the systems in a number of countries and also makes comparisons. His contribution to accounting education was referred to in the previous chapter. One of the most important and oft quoted recent research studies of the comparative case study type in international accounting is that by Zeff (1972) entitled "Forging Accounting Principles in Five Countries". This is an historical analysis of the development of the accounting principles in Canada, England, Mexico, Scotland and the USA. In the preface, Zeff explains that he believes that "enough countries have experience with programs designed to improve the quality of financial reporting that a comparison of their different approaches should be essayed". This he does and in his conclusion makes suggestions as to how the accountants in their particular countries and accountants in general could improve their approach to deciding on principles.

Zeff illustrates on a case by case basis how different forces have over time affected the development of accounting. Zeff does not attempt to say that the system in any one of these countries is similar to that to be found in any other country, and therefore that the lessons to be learned from the study of one country are applicable to other countries within a particular group. He does not suggest that the findings of any of these five case studies are capable of extention to other countries.

The AAA's 1974-75 Committee on International Accounting produced a very detailed descriptive study. The Committee had been asked to study the impact of different national accounting principles and practices on published financial statements by documenting the differences in a form suitable for use by other researchers. The annual report and accounts of six large companies were analysed in detail, the companies being one from each of six countries. The countries being Egypt, Sweden, Netherlands, West Germany, Switzerland and France. As expected the accounts vary very much in content and objective. "There are strong and weak aspects of financial reporting in all countries". The interesting point is made that it would "be quite useless to assume, as some critics have done that the unacceptable practices of one country are preferable to the unacceptable practices of another". By this they mean for example that the equity method of combining accounts is not superior or inferior to partial consolidation, nor the LIFO method of inventory valuation superior or inferior to other methods of creating hidden reserves.

As the AAA point out there is the danger that an author when making comparisons will make value judgements. Elliot (1968) in his book on accounting development in Latin America has as his objective "to bring to the interested reader a knowledge of accounting theory and practice in these countries; to compare their theory and practice with that which exists in the US; and where applicable, to suggest changes that will foster a greater standardisation of international accounting theory and practice, thereby permitting all users of financial statements to have a greater understanding of accounting data". The danger is that the changes suggested will be those that would benefit users in the writer's own country, rather than users in the country being studied.

Fortune in July 1962 criticised the financial accounting statements of European companies, specifically condemning the published data as inaccurate and unsuitable for proper financial analysis. Unfortunately the criticism was not particularly well informed. Most (1964) in "How Bad are European Accounts?" defends European accounting practices. He was replying to the article in Fortune. Most argued that it was possible to carry out meaningful financial analysis if one understood the differences between the countries. He agreed that differences in accounting and reporting practices did exist but said that these differences were not sufficiently large to prevent meaningful analysis. If one understood certain assumptions and postulates on which the accounts were based then one could make adjustments and this would lead to meaningful comparison.

This article of Most's was later criticised by Shillinglaw (1966) who found the conclusions of Most surprising. his first sentence makes the point that "it has long been taken for granted in the United States and perhaps in Great Britain that the annual financial statements and accounts of most continental companies are fundamentally different from and inferior to those of American and British firms". Most had argued that they were not inferior, just different. Shillinglaw was critical of the manipulation of hidden reserves, and of the lack of consolidation. He admits that skilled analysts such as Most could probably derive a great deal of information from European accounts as a result of reading them carefully, understanding the conventions that lie behind them and trying to form some judgement as to the basis of valuation and how conservative it has been. He goes on to say, however, that "the end result is bound to be unsatisfactory until some international agreement is achieved either on basic valuation standards or on the disclosure of enough data to permit the analyst to restate the published accounts on other and presumably more relevant bases".

Most replied to the Shillinglaw article in a letter published in Accountancy, May 1966. He repeats his conclusion that, with the exception of the unconsolidated accounts of holding companies, accounts prepared in different countries are meaningful and lend themselves to a degree of comparison. Shillinglaw had postulated a number of conditions which must be achieved before meaningful comparisons could be made. Most did not think that accounting practices had reached this degree of uniformity but still believes meaningful comparisons could be made. He pointed out that tax considerations and other arbitrary conventions are just as likely to dominate in accounts prepared in the USA as they are in France, Germany or the UK. He points out that on the question of price level changes Shillinglaw had mentioned that the Dutch were ahead in this practice and Most points out that French companies are also adjusting for inflation through the application of revaluation coefficients.

This debate which took place in the pages of a professional journal in 1966 is typical of disagreements which have taken place many times on this subject of comparability. Indeed comparability of accounts occupies a great deal of time of the European Federation of Financial Analysts who have been concerned since 1962 almost exclusively with measuring the difference between the accounting practices of countries and finding ways of dealing with these differences. Discussions on comparability also took place in Europe in the 1960s at the Congresses of the U.E.C.

Mueller (1972) discussed what he saw as the depressing state of accounting and financial reporting in Western Europe in the 1950s. He describes the different paths to greater disclosure in a number of these countries. Bedford and Gautier (1974) compare disclosure requirements in the EEC, Switzerland and the USA, and conclude that US requirements are wider than that in European countries, with the possible exception of the UK. This is of course not surprising as disclosure requirements to satisfy investors have not dominated accounting thinking in Europe as they have in the USA and the UK (Choi, 1973).

A classic work on comparison is that by Benston on "Public US compared to Private UK regulation of Corporate Financial Disclosure" (1976). This study deals with the difference in attitude that exists between the two countries. In the US there is a desire for public regulation whereas the UK wishes to continue with private rules. The private rules being found both in the Stock Exchange and the accounting profession. The paper explores the differences in the costs and benefits of the two systems. The author concludes that in his opinion private regulation is in many respects preferable. Not all would agree.

A particularly interesting comparative study was that by Davidson and Kohlmeier (1966), for not only did they describe the differences in certain accounting practices between the USA, the UK, France the Netherlands and Sweden, but they also measured how these differences affected financial statements, in particular the profit figures. They were concerned with the differences in the accounting for inventories and depreciable assets, and they prepared accounts for two US manufacturing businesses, adopting in turn the policies of each of the countries with respect to these two items. The results show that "stability of operations and of prices tend to narrow the effect of differences in accounting procedures". The spread in reported income figures is greater for the faster growing company. Another result was that it was the figures prepared according to the Swedish accounting practices that showed the widest departure from those of the other countries.

The authors comment on the often made point that differences in financial reporting methods from country to country are a restraint on the international flow of capital. "The unsatisfactory state of our present knowledge about the basis for investment decisions and capital movements prevents us from drawing any general conclusions. It is likely that assessments of income and risk as evidenced by the financial statements play some role in these decisions, perhaps a relatively important one. If this is so, some quantitative measures of the effects of international differences in accounting principles on significant financial statement items may, we hope, be helpful in moving toward more rational decisions in this important area". They are arguing for quantifying the effect of the difference, rather than for standardisation.

Whereas there have been numerous comparative studies that explain the differences between the methods of calculating profit in one country compared to another, there have been few studies that attempt to determine empirically the quantitative significance. This is an area which lends itself to empirical research and the lack of such studies is disappointing. Particularly so now that many large multinational companies are quoted on more than one stock exchange. It is often the case that they produce two or more statements, based on the accounting principles and practices of the countries in which they are quoted. The resulting differing profit and asset figures provide useful research material.

There have been quantitative comparisons. These include Davidson and Kohlmeier (1966) and Abel (1969) who did consider the significance of differences in profit measurement, but they based their analyses on simulated exercises, rather than on actual company data. The studies of Choi (1973) and Barrett (1975) (1976) were concerned with issues relating to the effect of the level of financial disclosure on the capital markets. Gray (1980) was concerned with the impact of differences in measuring profits in France, Germany and the UK, from a security analysis perspective. He found that large companies in the UK were relatively more optimistic in their measurement than were large companies in the other two countries.

Barrett (1976) was also interested in the effect of accounting reporting practices on capital markets. He points out that the capital markets of continential Europe have been shown to be less efficient than those of the USA and UK. Solnik and other financial researchers give as possible explanations for the low levels of efficiency in some capital markets, the financial practice in the countries concerned and the loose requirements for disclosure of information. Barrett's own study looks at two things. One being the overall level of financial disclosure and the second the degree of comprehensiveness of companies' financial statements. He analysed the annual reports of companies in seven countries. Not surprisingly he comes up with the finding that given the more advanced disclosure requirements in the UK and USA, the firms in these countries exhibited significantly more information in their reports than in the other five countries.

His overall conclusion was that, during the

period 1963 to 1972, although the level of corporate disclosure steadily improved there was still a wide variance between the level of disclosure of companies from the UK and USA on the one hand and those of companies in the five other countries on the other. The limits to drawing conclusions about market efficiency from the levels of disclosure is in fact recognised by Barrett. Published financial reports are only one way in which information is made available to investors. Unfortunately no alternative sources of financial information were examined. The close relationship, for example, between companies and banks in Germany which results in the exchange of information other than through accounting statements is not therefore taken into consideration.

The study by Singhvis (1968) and that by Qureshi (1975) illustrate the problems of inadequate disclosure in developing countries. Both studies based on the case study method show how important reliable and informative financial accounts are to a stock exchange. The papers are international in that in describing the problems of development in a particular country, they are providing guidance to investors and accountants in other countries.

A different type of research was that of Seidler (1969). He developed a model which relates the increasing aspirations of professional accountants to the quality of new entrants to the profession. He studied comparatively the social status of the accounting profession in the UK and USA, and reached the general conclusion that the profession generally enjoyed a higher status in the UK than in the USA.

The research that has been discussed up to this point in this section has been concerned with particular aspects of descriptive and comparative research. There are in addition a large number of articles and books that provide detailed factual descriptions of the accounting system or particular aspects of the accounting systems in individual countries or groups of countries. An early pioneering descriptive survey of professional accounting in a number of countries was that of the AICPA in 1964. This attracted a lot of attention and was referred to in numerous international accounting articles. They followed this up with a more extensive survey, published in 1975. The surveys that have provided data for a large number of studies are those of Price Waterhouse. These are major pieces of work that attempt very detailed analysis of accounting practices in a large number of countries. They are discussed in more detail later in this chapter. Other major surveys are those of Lafferty, Cairns and Carty (1979) and Lafferty and Cairns (1980).

The above surveys relate to the accounting practices of business enterprises. Enthoven (1970) concerned with all branches of accounting, provides a survey of the systems of uniform accounting that exist, making particular reference to the French, Belgian and German systems. In a later work Enthoven (1977) discusses accounting systems in developing countries and argues for introducing improved enterprise accounting within many such countries. This it is argued would make national economic planning very much easier and would therefore assist economic development. Enthoven explains that "various forms and methods of standardisation are feasible". Such standardisation (within a country) would "bring greater harmony, reliability, consistency and coordination of the system". He gives examples of three systems of standardisation that are available to Third World countries; namely the French 'Plan Comtable Général', the German framework of accounts (Kontenrahmen), and the GAAP, SEC, and Cost Accounting Standards Board of the USA.

Another type of comparative study is that of Stamp and Monitz (1978) who give details of the state of auditing standards in nine countries. A further type of comparative study is the survey of Bank Annual Reports produced by the Financial Times World Survey. The annual reports of the 100 largest international banks are analysed and compared. In the 1981 survey the top marks are given to the accounts of the Chase Manhatten Bank and the lowest marks to the accounts of the Credit Agricole Bank.

Lafferty (1975) and McClean (1973) have written on accounting practices and the accounting profession in European countries. Nobes and Parker (1981) include in their book detailed studies on accounting in seven countries, and a chapter on Accounting in Developing Countries. Extremely detailed reports are given on accounting in France and Germany in two books by Stillwell (1976), in Spain by Donaghy and Laidler (1981) and in Japan by Ballon, Tomita, and Usahi (1976). Elliot (1968), Rivera (1969), and Salas (1967), give details of the accounting profession in a number of South American countries.

The OECD's Committee on international investments and multinational enterprises, established an ad hoc Working Group on accounting standards. The Group produced a comprehensive survey of the accounting practices of its member countries (1980). The survey, which is based on the answers to a questionnaire, is particularly concerned with the existence and operation of accounting standards in individual countries. This survey was undertaken in order to assist the Group in its task of reviewing attempts to achieve harmonisation and advising the Committee on the desirability and feasibility of work by the OECD in this field of improving comparability.

A number of individual country studies focus on particular aspects of accounting. For example, the importance of the enterprise chamber on financial reporting in the Netherlands is discussed by Klaassen (1980). This is a method developed in that country for settling disputes between companies and parties interested in the financial statements. This innovation is obviously of interest to accountants in other countries. In fact accounting in the Netherlands has attracted much interest. Scott (1970) examines the Dutch replacement value discipline of business economics. He comments on the lack of interest up to that time in this approach outside the Netherlands, and believes this is because it is economic based. He states "Dutch accounting is likely to remain something of an enigma to American accountants". A typical comparative article was that of Frederiks (1974) which compares the regulations affecting the publication of annual reports in the Netherlands, with those in the USA and those of the Fourth EEC Directive. Macharzina and Coenenberg (1981) take an internationally based look at developments in inflation accounting. They refer to the fact that developments in Germany can be seen to be rather weak from the standpoint of British and North American inflation accounting proposals.

There are many such studies referring to practices in one country that it is thought will be of interest to an international audience. The ones referred to in the text are just to illustrate the approaches. To go into detail on all would read like a Cook's Tour for accountants. An excellent recent bibliography which gives details of articles on accounting standards and practices in selected countries and regions is that by Agami and Kollaritsch (1983). As has been indicated there are numerous comparative articles. Many of the early writings were clearly making a contribution to knowledge but one is forced to wonder whether some of the later works do add anything. The danger is that they either replicate the earlier work, coming out with the same results, or that their conclusion is what most people familiar with the subject would regard as obvious.

Barrett (1977) discusses the financial reporting practices in seven countries; the seven being arguably the most advanced private sector economies in the world, and concludes that financial disclosure has improved over the decade to 1972. With all the emphasis on improving disclosure standards in the late 1960s, this result is not really surprising. He also concluded that the level of disclosure by UK and US firms was "better" than in the other five nations.

Beazley (1968) argued that research is needed that focused upon the cross-cultural aspects of the operation of accountants in different environments. He points out that, when a businessman deals with a foreign counterpart, of a common economic and educational level, with whom he shares some perceptions, he may falsely assume that all of their perceptions are similar. He wants research to be undertaken that will "enable us to understand why people behave differently and to understand that difference is not necessarily synonymous with inferior". The objective is to "identify the variety of factors in the environment surrounding accounting would shape its character and the ways in which these factors vary in different settings". This was needed in 1968, it still is needed, this should be the objective of comparative research.

c) Classification (by observation)

The first question that will be considered is why classify? Nobes and Parker (1981) give four reasons. (i) "It should help to chart the progress of one system as it moves from one group to another, and the progress of ideas of a dominant country's system by noting the other nations systems grouped around it". The word progress implies that there is a hierarchy of systems. Change would be an alternative word. (ii) "In social sciences, classification may be used to help shape development rather than merely to describe how and why things are".

"For example, classification should facilitate a study of the logic of and the difficulties facing harmonisation". (iii) "Classification should also assist in the training of accountants and auditors who operate internationally". (iv) "A developing country might be better able to understand the available accounting systems and which one would be most appropriate (by studying a morphology) and seeing which other countries use particular systems".

Another reason advanced in the literature is that a country may be able to anticipate problems and consider possible solutions by observing what has happened in other countries with similar characteristics. However, there may be limits to the extent to which this is possible. Stamp (1980) believes that the USA approach to standard setting is not useful to Canada. He suggests that the future for Canadian standard setting should be significantly different from that for the USA. If this is generally the case it would reduce significantly the said benefits that can be obtained for one country by looking at what has happened in other countries - particularly if there are significant differences in two countries such as the USA and Canada that would appear to have so much in common. Not all agree with Stamp's argument. Boersema (1981) believes that Stamp exaggerates the differences, and that Canada should benefit from the work of the FASB: "A distinctive Canadian identity does not require an independent set of accounting principles".

Chetkovich (1972) also believes that "it is reasonable to expect that accountants in other countries will be able to benefit from our (USA) experience and thereby avoid some of the difficulties we have had". He does admit, however, that "in each country accounting should develop in a manner relevant to the society in which it exists".

It has been said there are four properties necessary in a good classification system. (See AAA 1977). First, the characteristics of a classification should be adhered to consistently. Secondly, there should be sufficient subsets to exhaust a given universe. Third, all subsets should be mutually exclusive, and finally hierarchial integrity should be observed. It is very hard to achieve these properties in the social sciences.

Two methodologies have been employed to determine clusters of countries, one being statistical analysis and the other subjective classifications, based on the descriptive literature. Both approaches assume that if similarity of the base is found (i.e. economic and/other environmental factors) then the countries will most probably use the same or closely related accounting practices.

An early analysis of accounting systems is that of Mueller (1967). As a result of considering the system in different countries he identifies four patterns of accounting.

a) Accounting within a macroeconomic framework

b) Microeconomic approach

c) Accounting as an independent discipline

d) Uniform accounting

Mueller believes there are only a few patterns of accounting development or 'cores' of accounting thought. The multiplicity of national accounting concepts and practices can be reduced to and explained in terms of these patterns or 'cores'. These patterns each have distinct fundamental premises, and therefore according to Mueller the diversity in international accounting is much less than that suggested by the descriptive literature. He expresses the hope that by highlighting different accounting patterns, and classifying these into groups, that it will be possible to link patterns of accounting development to accounting concepts.

Mueller (1967) classifies on the basis of differences in the role of accounting in the economic, governmental and business systems. In the first of his classifications accounting has developed to serve the needs of national economic policy; in the second of his groupings, accounting develops very much to serve the needs of individual private businesses, who want reality in measurements and valuations. The third group consists of countries where accounting has developed independently of government or micro-economic theories. The fourth group consists of countries where governments have used accounting as part of the administrative control of businesses, as opposed to using it for planning as in the first group.

In 1968 Mueller proposed a different method of classification. This is a classification of the business environment based on estimates of (a) the shades of political persuasion; (b) the reliance on the system of law; (c) the states of economic development; and (d) the stages of business complexity. He identifies ten different types of business environment. He was not in fact classifying accounting systems. However because the accounting system is a function of the business environment, he was advancing the hypothesis that countries with similar environments would have similar accounting systems.

Both of these Mueller studies are in fact producing classification based on influences. They are not classification of the actual accounting system. Another attempt to cluster countries based on dominant economic characteristics was that of Abu-Jbarah (1972). This study is also based on the assumption that a cluster of countries based on environments would be a reasonable guide to corresponding clusters based on accounting practices.

The AAA's Committee on International Accounting (1977) produced a classification of countries based on a number of states of society. At one extreme was the case of a political democracy, with its mass consumption, and with authority for accounting standards being in private hands, at the other extreme was the case of the traditional political oligarchy, underdeveloped, with few trained accountants, and decisions on accounting standards being in the hands of the executive. In between the extremes, three stages were identified. This morphology of accounting principles and financial reporting had originally been proposed by Buckley and Buckley (1974).

This again was not a classification of accounting systems, but a classification based on a number of parameters that were thought to be "pivotal to the type of accounting system which does (or can) emerge". The hypothesis that accounting systems would vary more between the different groups than it would between countries within a group was not tested with empirical data.

As well as this morphological approach to country systems the AAA's Committee (1977) also produced a 'subjective' classification based on zones of influence. They identified five different groups of countries, these being countries influenced respectively by the British, by either the French, Spanish or Portuguese, by the USA, by the Germans or Dutch, or by the Communist countries. Seidler in an earlier article (1967) had referred to 'Spheres of influence' and had identified three groups, three models of accounting systems. These were identified as the British model, the American

(USA) model and the Continental European model. Each model was based on a particular sphere of influence. Previts (1975) discussed these three models and classified a number of countries into one of these three models. He noted, for example, that major elements of the USA model had been adopted by Japan and Mexico.

Nobes and Parker (1981) produced a classification based on actual accounting practices. The classification of countries is based on their knowledge of the accounting practices of the countries and a discussion with experts. Not only do they classify countries into groups, they provide a theoretical framework for the breakdown. A hierarchial classification begins with a division between micro based and macro based systems. Subclasses are then produced based on such factors as the importance of business economic theories versus pragmatic business practices, and the importance of tax and legal matters rather than government economic plans. The 1981 book introduces the classification system. Nobes (1983) in a later article tests the model. The results will be discussed in the next section.

One large scale categorization of countries according to specific accounting practices or standards was that of Watt, Hammer and Burge (1977), in which 45 countries were examined. One part of the study dealt with the grouping of countries according to their audit requirements, and resulted in four clusters. The clusters varied from the group where all financial statements needed to be audited by independent public accountants, to a group where either there were no requirements or where requirements only applied to a limited number of companies. The second part of the study classified countries according to the "probability of fair presentation" of accounts. The word 'fair' was based on the UK/USA ideas of fair presentation.

One problem with most classification studies is that they take a static view of a country's accounting system. They look at the system at one point in time and try to establish patterns. Often the groupings so found are explained in terms of similar historical influences. The problem is that the accounting system of a country is usually changing, it is coming under different influences, and so groupings obtained at one point in time might not be the same as groupings found at another time. It is difficult therefore to use classification research to trace links in patterns of development.

The fact that usually the classification of a system is based on the system at one point in time is illustrated by Foroughi (1981). This study compares the accounting system in a country before and after a dramatic social change. The country he uses to illustrate the dramatic changes that can take place is Iran, whose accounting system he describes before and after the fall of the Shah.

Jusodirdjo (1979) illustrates the same problem and indicates a possible future difficulty. He points out that the accounting profession in Indonesia was very much influenced in its early days by the Dutch accounting system. However, with the influx of substantial investments from the USA the accounting profession adapted itself to economic changes by adopting US accounting ideas and practices. This initially caused problems as there was the dual accounting system. The Indonesian Accounting Institute have tried to resolve this by producing generally accepted accounting principles. These are "essentially patterned after the accounting and auditing principles and standards of the USA". Jusodirdjo welcomes the establishment of the South East Asia Federation of Accountants, seeing this as the first real step towards the attainment of standardisation of accounting principles in the region. But standardisation to meet S.E. Asian needs may mean Indonesia has to change from US theories and practices.

d) Classification (by Statistical Analysis)

Much of the recent comparative work which has been concerned with classification has made use of one of the newer statistical techniques. This work has been praised by some writers and criticised by others. Most of this research has made use of factor analysis to divide the countries of the world into different clusters. The clusters, the groupings of countries are in fact based on an analysis of the actual accounting systems.

In these statistical studies a number of accounting variables are used to divide countries into common groupings. The variables chosen on which to base the classification are either those that the researcher considers the most important or those that are thought more likely to be able to differentiate between groups. The countries are then divided into clusters on the basis of minimizing differences within groups and maximizing differences between groups. If meaningful groups can be identified, each group should exhibit greater uniformity in accounting practices within the group than exists between the groups.

Much of the accounting data in this statistical research is based on the survey and analysis of accounting practices in different countries produced by Price Waterhouse staff. The international survey was first published in 1973, with a second edition in 1975 and the results of a third survey published in 1979. The classification studies based on this survey data can be seen as either a comparatively easy way to undertake research, with the collection and summarising of the raw national data as the hard (time consuming) part; or alternatively they can be seen as the advanced part (requiring knowledge of statistical techniques) with the data gathering requiring less ability. A weakness, however, of the articles that base their conclusions on an analysis of the Price Waterhouse data, is that all the criticisms that apply to the basic data limit the significance of the conclusions. Clearly, these Price Waterhouse surveys represent mammoth and important pieces of work, but the reliability of some of the analysis has been challenged.

Nobes and Matatko (1980) analyse parts of the 1973 survey data and illustrate some of its misclassifications. For example, on the question of conservatism in accounts, the survey suggests "that UK and US accounting is similarly conservative to German accounting and actually more conservative than French accounting". This Nobes and Matatko say is misleading and results from the fact that "German and French conservatism is of a wholly different order to Anglo Saxon prudence". Other examples of problem areas are quoted in the 1980 article. Many of the problems with the Price Waterhouse 1973 survey data were corrected in the later surveys.

Nobes (1981) in a review of the 1979 publication challenges a number of points where he believes the survey is incorrect. One of these is the suggestion that International Accounting Standards are deemed mandatory in certain countries. In France in particular, he knows that it is not the case. In fact many of the international standards are contrary to the Law and established accounting practice in France. He finds problems in particular with I.A.S. 3 and I.A.S. 4 in that they are not used in France and the survey suggests that they are.

Nobes makes the point that some of the survey information should not be taken at its face value, and should not be thrown untouched into a computer in order to try and classify reporting systems by country. Further criticisms of the 1979 survey with respect to France appear in Nobes (1983).

Zeff (1980) drew attention to the possibility that the Price Waterhouse survey data may not be reliable with regard to some of the less developed nations. A similar point made is made by Nobes (1983). However having drawn attention to errors in some of the data Nobes (1982) does conclude that "whatever errors exist are probably minor and unsystematic". Goodrich (1982) points to the danger that little research would be undertaken if researchers refused to commence any study because of a slight weakness in the data. He also draws attention to the considerable efforts Price Waterhouse have gone to in order to make the data as reliable as possible.

The Price Waterhouse survey can be criticised but it is at the present time the best available attempt at a survey of the accounting practices in a large number of countries. The 1979 survey looks at 267 different accounting variables, ranging from depreciation policies to the treatment of extraordinary items, and it covers 64 countries.

Having discussed the data that is most often used in the statistical tests, the small number of statistical studies that have been undertaken will now be considered. Da costa, Bourgeois and Lawson (1978) examined 38 countries and considered one hundred relevant accounting practices. Highly correlated accounting practices were grouped together to give the variables to be used as the basis for classification. As a first step in the analysis countries were given a score, for each of these variables, according to whether the practice was not permitted, was followed by a minority, one half, a majority, or compulsory. As the second step, a principal components factor analysis was carried out. The third step was grouping the countries by the similarity of these factors. "Two clusters were discerned - each an international grouping in which member countries exhibited a homogeneity". The financial accounting practices of one group are strongly related to practices in the UK. The other group is harder to explain. The USA appears to the researchers to be the group leader, but the group contains France and Germany, and it is doubtful if influential members of the business and accounting communities in these countries would like to consider they are following USA practices. The article is an interesting example of the use of the research technique, but the authors have problems explaining their results. Nobes and Parker (1981) claim one reason for the problems lies in poor screening of the original data, it was in fact based on the first of the Price Waterhouse surveys, that of 1973, and in that survey there appear to have been problems in classifying accounting practices.

Frank (1979) used the same 1973 survey data. In this study, a variant of factor analysis, namely multiple discriminant analysis, was used to identify groups of countries which share similar accounting concepts and practices. "Data on the extent of usage of 233 different accounting principles and reporting practices in 38 non-communist countries were analysed for this purpose". The research identified four factor groupings. These four groupings "have an intuitively appealing interpretation as prototype or accounting models".

The names assigned to the groups were the British Commonwealth Model, Latin American Model, the Continental European Model, and the United States Model. It is interesting that this conforms closely with the models resulting from the subjective research of the AAA (1977) and Seidler (1967), except that in the Frank study a Latin American model is identified as distinct from the US model. Frank discusses the strength and weaknesses of his research, and concludes that "the results of discriminant analysis tend to provide strong support for the propositions advanced by international accounting theorists that cultural and economic factors are associated with the particular set of accounting principles and practices used by various countries". Undoubtedly true, but a worrying thought for those advocating international accounting standards.

This work of Frank was extended in a later article, (Nair and Frank 1980), in which the 1975 Price Waterhouse survey data (sometimes referred to as the 1976 data) was used in addition to the 1973 data. In this later research, groupings of countries were obtained based on disclosure practices and groupings also obtained based on measurement practices. The groupings obtained on the basis of one set of factors were found to be different from the groupings obtained using the other set. This result is worrying for those who hope to be able to classify countries into groups, it showed that the groupings "achieved on different subsets of accounting practice are in fact different". One of the properties necessary for a good classification system is that the characteristics of a classification should be adhered to consistently. Accounting classifications do not appear to be doing this.

A second question considered by the Nair and Frank research is "whether different economic and cultural variables were associated with each subset of practices". The variables considered included measures designed to disclose the structure and type of economy and the trading affiliations of each country. It was found that the two subsets yielded very different results. The specific variables most closely related to each subset were different. The authors make the point that "because of these differences, it may be more difficult for policy makers to achieve harmonization of accounting practices than was previously realized".

Nobes and Parker (1981) produce a hypothetical classification of accounting systems. It is subjective. They mention that they plan to empirically test their hypothesis. In fact in a research paper Nobes and Matatko (1980) do empirically test the hypothetical classification of Nobes and Parker. They discuss the hypothesis and test it making use of the 1973 and 1975 Price Waterhouse data. All the variables measured in the two surveys are utilised; they use a similar statistical method to that of da Costa et al (1978) namely to cluster countries on the basis of similarity in accounting practices. They discuss a number of statistical problems that arise in this type of work. For example the Price Waterhouse data is qualitative, countries are given an ordinal 'score' for each practice examined. In fact the scores are not values on a continuous scale. This leads to difficulties in interpreting the results. There are other statistical problems, some of which Nobes and Matatko try to correct.

They find that their empirical results conflict with those of da Costa et al. They used a larger data base, but did not find this had any significant effect. They did not find it as easy to use their resulting correlation coefficients to find clusters of countries as did da Costa et al. They could in fact only identify two groupings, one cluster for countries coming under UK influence, and one for those not. "The inability to allocate a large number of countries including the US and Germany to clusters is a strong negative result".

Surprisingly a division of countries between those with US influence and those with a Continental European influence was not possible from the data used and the statistical techniques employed. They suggest further study is needed.

Goodrich (1982) discusses the comparative studies that have used factor analysis and points out that "depending on the factor analytic technique options chosen, the variables included and the survey year, each of these researchers has found slightly different groupings. The bulk of the countries are classified similarly by the factor analysts. Certain countries such as Canada and the Netherlands are more difficult to place and are, in fact, sorted into different groupings in different studies. The US and the UK were never placed by any of these studies in the same category. Mexico was always grouped with the US".

Goodrich has argued that the use of factor analysis as an inductive process is particularly relevant in the field of international accounting since it simplifies and explores a very complex field. Goodrich reports the results of his study using factor analysis. He uses a slightly different statistical technique to that used by Frank, and da Costa et al., the technique used recognises linkages between groups, and does not posit completely separate groups. His results indicate five groups. One group comprises nations in the sphere of influence of the US, a second group 'has a distinctly Latin flavour', a third group includes the UK, a number of countries that are or were members of the British Commonwealth plus a few other countries including France and Belgium, a fourth group includes India, Australia, Japan and Brazil, and the fifth group consists of a very strange mixture of countries.

It is of course possible to undertake statistical research that classifies countries without using the Price Waterhouse data base. It is possible to study in detail for each country the factors that are important in differentiating between the accounting systems of countries. The selected data can then be used as an input in the analysis. It probably means that less countries will be covered by the analysis but it means that the data being used is reliable and relevant to the particular study. This was the approach adopted by Nobes (1983), in the research which tested the model developed by Nobes and Parker (1981).

Descriptive, Comparative and Classification

The model of Nobes and Parker was used to predict which countries would be grouped together based on their respective measurement and valuation practices. The predictions relating to 14 countries were tested. The data used to classify was obtained as a result of visits, interviews and reading relating to each of the countries. This type of classification study is based on detailed case studies about each country. It is based partly on judgement and partly on statistical analysis. For each factor considered important in differentiating between countries a score is given for each country. For example one of the factors considered in the Nobes study was the consolidation practice of the country. A score was given depending on whether the practice was rare,was sometimes carried out, was practiced in relation to domestic subsidiaries only, or was always required. Statistical analysis is then used to place the countries in clusters. The results show a clear split between those accounting systems that are micro based and those that are macro based. The further division into sub classes also shows encouraging results.

Classification based on factor analysis has been criticised. One problem is that the hypotheses that have so far been advanced have related to classifications of influence on accounting rather than classification of actual accounting systems. A further problem is that more thought needs to be given to the theories of accounting, to the different methodologies. What are the characteristics of the different models of financial accounting? This needs to be considered before the classification stage. The models need to be developed before the classification stage.

The empirical testing has made use of the Price Waterhouse data; and the analysis is based on the assumption that the variables included in the survey are a reasonable model of international reporting principles and policies. There are, however, other variables that might have been included. We have not developed models to explain why certain countries have similar patterns or to explain which variables should be looked at to decide if they are similar.

Finally it must be recognised that a classification of systems is only good for one moment in time. The systems are changing over time, as can be seen from the changes in most countries accounting principles and practices over the last ten years. The classifications show the position at just one point in time. Case studies often show why and how a particular country adopted its accounting system and practices. It would be interesting to consider how these practices are likely to change.

It is easy to criticise any empirical research. These studies using factor analysis are a step forward from the descriptive type of comparative article and do contribute to our knowledge of international accounting. They are an attempt to undertake rigorous research in a very difficult area.

Chapter Four

HARMONIZATION AND/OR STANDARDIZATION

a) Introduction

The main interest in accounting at the present time at the domestic level appears to be the formulation of accounting standards. Baxter (1981) sees this as a phase in the development of accounting. With national accounting standards being created there is a natural interest at the international level in harmonizing accounting practices. If it is possible to standardise an accounting practice within a country, why should this standard not also be applicable in another country. This can be seen as a phase in the development of international accounting. The introduction of standards that can be applied in more than one country being the latest aspect in the spread of ideas.

This chapter is divided into a number of parts. The introduction will consider what is meant by terms such as harmonization and standardisation. Part b) traces the development of the harmonization debate. In part c) the arguments that have been advanced for harmonization will be examined. In part d) the literature on the setting of international accounting standards is considered covering who should set and enforce such standards. In part e) the arguments against harmonization and international standards are reviewed. Finally in part f) the role of the supra-national agencies and international bodies concerned with harmonization and increased levels of disclosure will be considered.

In Chapter One reference was made to a number of branches of accounting. This chapter is mainly concerned with harmonization at the micro accounting level, in particular at the enterprise level. It should not be forgotten, however, that international harmonization has in most respects been achieved at the macro accounting level. The need for standards in national income accounting was much discussed in the literature before the second world war. From 1953 the OECD began to publish national income accounts for its member countries based on a standardised system. At the same time the United Nations decided to set up a standard system of its own that would enable comparable national income accounts to be produced. In 1956 the two systems were merged (UN 1953). The United Nations have also produced a manual on Governmental Accounting. There is an excellent survey article by Stone (1981) on the international harmonization of National Income accounts. There may be lessons to be learned from the process by which such harmonization was achieved for those trying to introduce some degree of harmonization in the financial accounts of enterprises. The arguments advanced for harmonization are similar in both branches of accounting. It was the supra-national agencies and international bodies that wanted harmonization in national income accounts and it was they who had the necessary authority to bring it about. It must be stated however that although there is now an agreed format for national income accounts there are wide differences in the level of reliability of different countries accounts.

Returning to enterprise accounts the first thing that has to be decided is what is the issue being discussed. Is it international uniformity, international standards or international harmonization? These three words are continually appearing in the literature, but are not always defined.

Uniformity - is a condition in which everything is regular, homogeneous or unvarying. It implies sameness, and in this context means that all accounting principles and practices are the same. Enthoven (1967) refers to the American Accounting Association definition of uniformity as "consistent classification and terminology as well as consistent measurement".

Standards - are an authorised model of a unit of measure. So attempts in accounting to standardize are attempts to introduce uniformity in accounting methods. The model that is to be used for measurement being the authorised version.

Harmonization - is the attempt to bring together different systems. It is a process of blending and combining various practices into an orderly structure, which produces "synergistic result" (Miller 1979). It first involves examining and comparing the different accounting systems in order to note points of agreement and disagreement, and then working towards bringing these different systems together. Those who believe that uniformity is desirable, would as a first step, need to compare the different systems, then they would need to persuade others that some measure of agreement would be advantageous, they would then work towards harmonization, attempting over time to remove differences. They would be working towards the acceptance of some authorised model, a set of standards. When this had been achieved there would be uniformity.

The steps in the process would therefore, according to the normal usage of the words appear to be: comparison > move towards harmonization > producing agreed standards > uniformity. It is possible of course to stop at any point in this process.

Nobes and Parker (1981) point to this problem of definition. They define 'harmonization' as the process of increasing the compatability of accounting practices by setting bounds to their degree of variation. 'Standardization' they see as implying the formation of a more rigid set of rules. They explain however that within accounting these words have taken on technical meanings and therefore "one cannot rely upon the normal differences in their meanings. For example, the EEC in moving towards transnational legislation refer to the process as one of "harmonization". In practical terms harmonization within the EEC will be much more powerful and important than the standardisation of the IASC". Harmonization does not imply complete standardisation. It is the process of reducing differences. Nobes (1980) does not see the harmonization within the EEC as meaning "uniform and rigid rules throughout the EEC".

As well as considering the arguments for and against harmonization, we need to consider various intermediate positions. There are many that argue that rigid uniformity would be undesirable, that it is necessary to allow for the different economic, social and political conditions of a country. Mueller in his early book on International Accountinf (1967) pointed out that "on the whole complete international uniformity seems undesirable, especially if the different development patterns are taken into account.... Significantly different environmental circumstances are not conducive to singular international accounting uniformity. Yet certain sectional and national development patterns based on a uniform approach are clearly in evidence". It is interesting that he made these comments when discussing attempts by the UEC in the 1950s to introduce "uniform charts of accounts".

If uniformity is not considered desirable but some degree of harmonization is considered necessary, this leaves various possibilities. For example, only harmonise on non-controversial aspects, or produce two sets of accounts, one conforming to internationally agreed standards and one to satisfy national needs. These proposals will be considered later.

A division can be made between the idea of international accounting standards and the idea of harmonization of accounting practices. Choi (1973) (1974) and others see international accounting standards as helping to meet the needs of international investors, which would help in the movement of funds around the world.
Others, however, see international accounting standards as ready-made standards suitable for adoption for any country in the world. The IASC itself sees the standards very much in that role as they are urging member countries or to be more accurate urging member organisations in these countries to try to have IASC standards adopted.

b) The Development over time of the Harmonization and Standardization Debate

In recent years a lively debate has taken place in the literature, particularly in the professional literature on the subject of harmonization of accounting practices across countries. The pressure for harmonization has increased, and there are now in existence international accounting standards, and committees at an international level, both public and private, looking into the possibilities of further harmonization of standardization.

From the beginning of this century, the interest in the possibilities of harmonization have been growing. Not surprisingly the large international accounting firms have been concerned about the number of different practices they encounter. Within Price Waterhouse, between 1901 and 1913, there were exchanges of views between the British and the USA branches of the firm on the subject of group accounts (Kitchin 1972). A partner in the firm, Garnsey, was an important man in these discussions; he later wrote on the issues involved (1923). In 1924, Dickinson, another partner in Price Waterhouse, lectured in London on this subject (see Kitchin 1972).

The increasing interest of the profession in possible harmonization has been reflected in the proceedings and discussions of the international congresses. The first accounting congress at which accountants from different countries came together in 1904, did not devote much time to discussing differences; there was only one comparative paper. The objectives of the 1904 congress have been considered by Previts (1975), Mueller (1979) and Samuels (1985). It would seem that the main objective was to increase the status and unite the profession in the USA, international issues were not important.

The Accounting Congress held in St. Louis in 1904, was part of the Worlds Fair that was being held in that city at the time. In fact it was common practice at that time for international exhibitions and fairs to offer meetings for intellectual and professional bodies. The 1900 Paris Exposition attempted to launch an International Association of Science, Arts and Education. At the 1910 Brussels Exposition, an international accounting meeting was held, entitled the World Congress of International Associations. The Belgium based Association Internationale de Comptabilité (AIC) took on the responsibility for organising these World Congresses, and ten had been held by 1939.

Little is written about these Congresses or the Association. This is unfortunate for the papers presented are of relevance today. In preparation for the 1910 meeting a survey was undertaken into the problems arising from non-standardised accounting. (See Mommen 1961). At the second congress held in 1911 comparative accounting theory and practices were discussed including triple entry bookkeeping as practised in Russia. At the third congress held in 1913, universal schemes of coding of accounts were discussed. At the fifth congress, held in 1926, there were plans discussed to expand nationally based accounting into one system to serve a world economy. (For a discussion on these congresses see Forrester 1984.) It can be seen from the topics discussed that these AIC organised meetings were very much international in flavour. The topics are still with us today.

A meeting which was called the second International Congress was held in Amsterdam in 1926. There were accountants present from 17 countries. The Congress had, among its objectives, "the offer of the opportunity for an international exchange of views regarding subjects which concern accountancy and efficiency and thereby hopes to work towards international rapprochement in order ... to further the mutual acquaintance with, and the uniformity of the method of, accountants in various countries ... and to propagate views that can be adopted internationally regarding problems concerning the science of cost calculation and the princples of efficiency".

The form of sessions adopted at this 1926 meeting was to be followed at later congresses; representatives from different countries were asked to speak on a topic of common interest and so highlight the similarities and differences between the methods adopted in the countries of the speakers. Here were the comparative papers which have occupied so much of the literature in international accounting. There was an interesting comparative paper given by R.H. Montgomery from the USA. He adopted the technique, unfortunately followed by speakers at later conferences, of going through a number of countries in alphabetical order. Starting with Argentina, he moved to Australia, Belgium, British India, China and so on. This paper was followed by a discussion on the differences in legislation between countries. Montgomery disagreed with Plender on the need for legislation and on the need for more than one accounting body in any country. A paper was also given on education for the profession.

Whilst the Congress was taking place a meeting was held of the representatives of the accounting organisations from the different countries. The Chairman introduced this working session by saying that it was the most important meeting of the week, as decisions would have to be taken that were most important for the accounting profession. They had to decide in principle whether it was desirable to establish a permanent committee for the organisation of international congresses. The representatives present agreed that they needed to go back to their national associations to see if they had their support. There was a consensus on the need to hold such conferences in the future. Mr. Van Dien from the Netherlands (who had turned up unexpectedly at the St. Louis Congress in 1904) and who was the driving force behind the 1926 congress was appointed

Chairman of the organising committee.

At the time of this second congress an article appeared in The Accountant, 2nd October 1926 written by P.D. Leake suggesting that in view "of the great and growing importance of the accounting profession throughout the world, and the many subjects of international concern with which accountants have to deal, it is suggested that the time may be near for the formation of an International Accountants Association, somewhat on the lines of the International Law Association". He suggested that meetings of the International Accountants Association might well be open not only to accountants but also to those engaged in world industry and commerce, the idea being that anybody interested in questions involving international accounting should be welcome to attend. He continued to draw analogies between the International Law Association and the one proposed. He pointed out that in his opinion the responsibilities of the accountant are as onerous and important as those of a lawyer. He spoke highly of the International Conference in Amsterdam and mentioned how valuable it was in allowing accountants from different lands to get together. The object of the congress was to give opportunity for international exchange of views and he hoped that the regular interchange of views would do much to advance the science of accountancy. He pointed out that there was still much work to do.

Things do not seem to have changed very much over the last 60 years. In reply to Leake's suggestion a letter was published making the point that there was a lack of national cooperation and coordination in accounting and until this had been achieved what hope was there for international agreement. While it was agreed that there was a vast, almost unexplored field of problems in accounting needing solutions, it was thought that much more might be done to solve these problems by the formation of District and National Associations in order to crystallise geographical and national views.

In an Editorial in The Accountant (7th July 1926) the opinion is expressed that the profession should as far as possible grow up along the same lines in all countries. Uniformity in such matters as ethics and educational standards is essential and this can only be attained by international cooperation. The second point that is made is that there is no better way of cultivating a broad and liberal view than by exchanging ideas with those whose outlook may be influenced by different racial and national characteristics, and who may accordingly throw fresh light on the problem by viewing it from a different angle. The third point that is made is that international intercourse such as international congresses help in working towards world peace.

For the third international congress (or possibly the second!) the profession moved in 1929 back across the Atlantic to New York; this turned out to be a very large congress and sixty-five papers were presented. There were representatives from seventeen countries and the opening paper was given by E. Van Dien on the development of professional accounting in Continental Europe. There were eleven country papers given on the topic of "Legislation and Education for the Accounting Profession". There were papers on consolidated financial statements given by speakers from the UK and USA.

There were many disappointing aspects of the congress; there was a paper on accounting in Continental Europe that followed the procedure of just listing the practices in one country followed by the practices in another country. There was a paper given by a famous economist, Irving Fisher, a Professor at Yale. He was arguing for standardisation but standardisation of the calendar. There was a strong movement at the time for calendar reform, it was being proposed that the world adopt a thirteen month calendar. The League of Nations had become involved. Numerous national committees had been set up to investigate the possibilities. Fisher was a big supporter of the idea; he concluded, "It may be said with emphasis, that the advantages of stabilising the unit of time far outweigh its disadvantages and would bring simplicity and added efficiency into the economic and household affairs of the world". A strange topic for an international accounting congress. It is perhaps unfair to draw a parallel with the present debate on standardising accounting, but similar claims were being made for standardising the calendar as are now being made for international accounting standards.

One of the earliest appeals for standardisation appears in a paper given by Professor Kester of Columbia University at the third international congress (1929). He argued for standardisation at an international level. He said, "As our civilisation grows more complex, it becomes more and more difficult to understand and interpret properly".

"A great saving will accrue as a result of the further extension of the standardisation movement into the field of business records and reports. It is, of course, recognised that the development of uniform and standard accounting methods must take cognizance of the legal requirements and restrictions of the various countries". He recognised that standardisation would have to take into account different economic and social backgrounds. The reasons why he thought standardisation was desirable was a) it would result in a saving of time and effort by accountants, b) it would lead to sounder accounting methods in many countries, and c) it would lead to more reliable and trustworthy data. This paper in 1929 by Kester has been rewritten many times since, with different authors names appearing. An interesting point was made in the discussion of the standardisation paper; a Mr. Eaton, President of the New Jersey Society of C.P.A.s said, "It is not for the accountants....but it is for the accountants and businessmen, the lawyers, the economists and all others who read and use balance sheets (this includes Profit and Loss Accounts), to gather together into a common language those expressions which are needed in order for a common understanding". He was making the point that it was not just up to accountants to be involved in standards; again an often repeated point.

Perhaps the outstanding paper from an academic point of view was that presented by Professor Schmidt of the University of Frankfurt who was the leading authority in the world on inflation accounting. He presented a paper on the valuation of fixed assets in financial statements. He stated that "Valuation according to original purchase price does not hold good over a period when the level of values is changing". After a discussion, Schmidt concluded, "It seems to me that present day valuation is getting more friends from congress to congress, though it is by no means fully recognised. If once the accounting profession accepts the principle, there will be much research work to develop practical methods of calculation on the basis of present-day costs and for this purpose the work of German writers on the subject may be of help to our American brethren". The extent to which the American brethren and the British brethren took notice of Schmidt was, however, limited.

The Fourth Congress was held in London in July 1933; a number of important international issues were discussed, for example, international finance, and currency exchange rate fluctuations in relation to subsidiary company accounts. An important paper was given by Lord Plender in which he said, "The accounting problems to be considered at this Congress cover a wide area and the application of the principles involved is in many respects international. But it must be remembered that the laws of the countries differ and to expect international uniformity in all these respects is impractical". The same point had been made at previous conferences and has been made many times since. In an International Finance paper given by Sir Josiah Stamp, he pointed to the urgent problems (emphasis on the word 'urgent') that result from using money as a measure of value. He was concerned that traditional methods ignored fluctuations in price levels: "Accountancy conventions lead to a depreciation of stock (share price) values".

The last pre-Second World War Congress was held in Berlin in September 1938. This was quite a remarkable conference as photographs of the delegates attending the meetings reveal. A large number of very well dressed accountants stand beneath large flags. The hosts for the congress, clearly wished to use the international meeting for political purposes. They appreciated the value of these congresses as a means of spreading ideas! Following the welcoming address the President of the English Institute, Charles Palmour, spoke and expressed the thanks of the foreign delegates. He said, "Gatherings of this character afford the opportunity for the interchange of views on the many problems of practice by which the accounting profession is confronted". In a clever speech, he makes reference to the fact that whatever the differences in our politics, no one can dispute that 2 + 2 = 4.

Following the Second World War came attempts to create a greater degree of international cooperation, both at a political and economic level. There were suggestions that an 'International Institute of Accountancy' be formed under the aegis of UNESCO. The founder of the UEC, Paul Caujolle, was afraid such an institute could not be effective because the stages of development of the profession in different parts of the world were too divergent. Better, in his opinion, to limit the institute "to European countries which had reached a comparable stage of economic legal and technical evolution". (See Fain 1961).

Caujolle seeking to harmonise the profession in Europe arranged a meeting that brought together at Basle in March 1951 representatives of a number of professional bodies from European countries. As a result a Union (UEC) was set up with three aims, one cultural, one to engage in technical studies, and one to promote student exchange. In 1953 the first congress of the UEC (Union Européenne des Experts Comptables Economiques et Financiers) was held in Italy. The theme of the congress was "Accounting Uniformity and Economic Integration". A permanent commission was set up to investiage the feasbility of introducing a 'European Uniform Chart of Accounts'. This reflected the interest of a number of European countries in uniform accounts. Uniform accounts had been introduced nationally, and so the question arose of uniform system across a number of countries which had strong economic links.

A UEC committee on terminology and accounting interpretation reported in 1958. They had spent a number of years trying to find a common ground with respect to accounting methods and procedures. The results were regarded by Engelmann (1962) as 'meagre'. The European Union in its attempts to bring together the different European practices, found it necessary to prepare a UEC Lexicon, a guide to the meaning of terms in different languages. The UEC has "undoubtedly pioneered agreement on basic accounting matters" (Accountancy Editorial, October 1980). The emphasis is on basic however, for the article goes on to say, "it would seem optimistic to hope for any major contribution to the more sophisticated issues".

The interest in international harmonization continued to grow. A valuable paper on the evolution of international accounting standards is that of Mason (1981). Jacob Kraayenhof is often mentioned in the literature as the 'father of the movement'. In 1957 he had been President of the 7th International Congress of Accountants held in Amsterdam. He presented a paper at the 1959 annual meeting of the American Institute of CPA's which was published in 1960. He was not advocating rigid uniformity; he supported the widest possible acceptance amongst countries "of a set of ... rules, which for certain items may be broad and differing". He recognised, however, that on some issues, difference of opinion may be so great that agreement could not be reached, and wanted loose uniformity with agreed standards on some items, but flexibility on others.

Kraayenhof (1960) argued strongly for some degree of international uniformity on accounting principles. "What good reasons can be given, other things being equal, for adopting different principles in various countries as to the valuation of stocks, as to methods of depreciation etc ..." This argument is based on the assumption "other thing being equal". Unfortunately, they very rarely are. As Kraayenhof goes on to say that "when selecting one of the various alternatives offered by a set of rules, the choice in any given country is determined by other than purely economic factors, e.g. prevailing political risks or geographical conditions. But the basic principles underlying the financial presentation in each case should be the same".

The Ninth International Conference (1962) included a session on the harmonization of accounting principles. This session reflected the increasing interest in the subject. There were ten country papers all indicating problem areas in the way of harmonization. T. Cowan chaired the session, his paper dealt with the accounting diversity that existed throughout the world. He commented upon, amongst other things, secret reserves and how practices on this issue vary from country to country. The paper presented by the Swedish delegate on the subject led Cowan to conclude that the significance of external financial reporting is related closely to the sources of business finance. Where banks are the major providers of finance secret reserves may be less objectionable than in situations where there is a well established capital market with the constant buying and selling of a company's shares. The relevance of the financial system was dealt with by a number of delegates. The condoning of secret reserves was seen not just as a case of accounting principles but as the product of historical and current factors within a society of a quite complex kind. They were of course discussing the economic and social problems that stand in the way of harmonization.

Karen, another speaker at the Ninth Congress, believed that the congress should recognise the need for the formulation and acceptance of a statement of broad accounting objectives. Because there was a need for assembling and exchanging knowledge and experience in accounting as a means to the development of a common international approach, he recommended the setting up of an international bureau for accounting research, information and cooperation. Although speaking in favour of harmonization, he was not unaware of the problems. One of the points he made was that individual states cannot be expected to forego their legislative powers in the interests of international uniformity in the field of financial reporting. However, looking towards the future he could see the move towards internationalism in business and the various trading blocs, such as the EEC, leading the way towards harmonization.

The organisers of the conference suggest in an explanatory statement that it is necessary to elaborate the principles and standards of international coverage which would be freely accepted by accountants. Karen makes the point that this will be difficult to achieve when the accountants of a single country are unable to agree on quite basic issues. "The profession in each country should continue to define accounting principles and objectives and to relate these to accounting and auditing practices so as to raise standards and reduce diversity". Karen believes that "The international harmonization of accounting is certain to be a long process". "It seems neither practical nor desirable to aim at a rigid international code of accounting terminology". One difficulty in achieving rigid uniformity being that language differences meant that words are given different meanings in different countries.

The French speaker on this topic, Lauzel, makes two interesting points. He states that however far accounting standardisation may be taken there will always be elements of disparity which cannot be eliminated. He indicates that fiscal legislation would be one particular element that would lead to differences. He points out that accounting standardisation of the kind undertaken in France to meet the needs of economic planning runs the risk of going against the ethics of free enterprise in a market economy. He hopes that it would be possible to accept an intelligent compromise between the need for discipline inherent in defending the citizens rights (the French legal approach) and a need for freedom quite legitimately felt by those who want to adapt accounting to the needs of good and responsible management.

There were two other sessions at the Ninth Congress covering international issues, one on the harmonization of auditing standards and procedures and the other on accounting problems peculiar to international enterprises. There was even a fourth session covering an international aspect namely a group of papers coming under the collective title "Decisive factors governing investments as from one country to another". The Ninth Congress clearly reflected the increasing interest in general in international accounting and in particular in the harmonization process. The papers point to the many problems that have since been encountered and have since been written about numerous times.

Another important stage in the development of the international aspects of accounting was the publication in 1964 by American Institute of CPA's "Professional Accounting in 25 countries". This book was written by staff of Price Waterhouse, reflecting the international involvement of the firm, the book turned out to be an important source of data for a number of empirical research studies.

Returning to the UEC, W.E. Parker, representing the English Institute, spoke at the Fifth UEC Congress in 1964 pointing out that he found it difficult to comment on the proposal under discussion for a European Plan of Accounts, as the UK had no national plan and had never thought of having one. "To the British, accounting attempts to standardise on a uniform national scale, let alone on an international scale ... seem to be fraught not only with difficulties but with dangers". The dangers he believed, that would be seen by most British accountants, would be that the plan, if it was effective, would not be sufficiently flexible to accommodate varieties and changes of circumstances. The "adoption of the plan would produce a superficial appearance of uniformity which would be deceptive in as much as, while the amounts shown by the accounts would be classified under uniform headings, the principles on which the amounts were arrived at might differ greatly". The British preferred to seek greater uniformity of accounting principles, allowing flexibility in classification and presentation.

Mueller (1972) makes reference to "the start of the international disclosure bandwagon circa 1965". He mentions that in the 1960s the US accounting literature did not reflect much of an interest in the subject of international disclosure which was "gathering steam" in other countries. However, occasional references were made in the literature to "an international trend to broader disclosure" (see Lybrand Newsletter, 1966).

Sir Henry Benson provides a very personalised account of the movement to establish international accounting standards. He explains how, after the

1939-45 war, he "began to realise that a degree of uniformity in accounting matters was not only desirable but necessary" At the time he was "Helping to build up my firm's national and international accounting practice", and he "realised that it would be quite impossible to do so without clear manuals of procedure and principles for the guidance of partners and staff world wide".

In 1966 proposals were made to set up a three-nation study group (UK, USA and Canada) to compare the current trends in accounting thought and practices in the member countries. Initially the emphasis was to be on comparison. Sir Henry suggested at the time that agreed statements be issued on major accounting problems. He saw this as one way of promoting international cooperation in accounting. He suggested that either similar study groups might be organised with accounting organisations in other countries or that the original group might be expanded.

The Accountants International Study Group (AISG) was formed in 1966. It was minuted that "if AISG proved to be a success, other nations might be invited to join later on". One aim of the group was to help to enhance international cooperation within the accounting profession. A number of comparative studies were produced by the group. In one of them on 'International Financial Reporting' (1975) it recommended that multiple sets of statements, primary and secondary, should usually be prepared for an enterprise with a financial reporting audience in more than one country. The primary reports being to satisfy users needs in the company's country of domicile, with secondary reports being prepared to meet the needs of audiences-of-interest in other countries in which the company operated.

This is the suggested solution of one school of thought to the problem of transnational financial reporting. It clearly does not require international standards. The study group did consider the possibility of a set of generally accepted international reporting standards which "would not be bound by the social, political or economic influences of any one country". But they believed that the likelihood of countries being able to agree to any one set of standards in the near future was small and therefore that particular solution to the reporting problems was not very reasonable.

Savoie (1969) describes how a Working Party that was formed at the Ninth International Congress went about improving international accounting communications. This Working Party, together with the work of the Accountants International Study Group, he saw as encouraging signs that real progress was being made towards the international development of the accounting profession and the harmonization of accounting principles. Thomas (1970) discusses the work of the IASG over its first three years.

At the Tenth International Congress of Accountants held in Sydney in 1972, representatives of the profession in the UK, USA and Canada met and proposed that an international body should be set up which would write accounting standards for international use. There was further discussion on this topic later in 1972 and professional bodies from six other nations were invited to join the organisation. It was thought that an international organisation with less than 9 member countries would be unworkable, and would be unrepresentative from an international point of view. The inaugural meeting of the resulting International Accounting Standards Committee was held on 29th June 1973. It was intended that the IASC would produce basic standards that would be capable of rapid acceptance and implementation worldwide.

Once it had been formed many other countries applied to join the Committee because as Benson (1976) explained it helped them keep up to date in relation to international accounting matters and it saved them the heavy cost in time and money of writing standards of their own.

Benson (1976) wrote that "I know that the standards so far issued (up to 1976) ... are not perfect. Sometimes they reflect a compromise, or proffer alternatives; sometimes they may not be penetrating enough. Nevertheless they are a gallant start. Any attempt to have moved too quickly or too fast in the formative years would have been fatal. I think IASC has come to stay and that its impact will increase in the years to come. I have never thought that the impact of IASC will be revolutionary or immediate ... the impact will be important in the next 10 years and of dominating importance in the presentation of financial statements by about the year 2000".

Hayes (1980) who at the time was the US representative in the IASC, points out that the committee will soon "have covered most of the areas of accounting dealt with in the professional literature in the United States". He sees this as the end of the first stage of its work, the second phase will be "to continue to narrow alternative practices".

Another international body, the International Federation of Accountants (IFAC) had been founded in 1977, just prior to the 11th International Congress. It began with a membership of professional accounting bodies from 49 countries. Its programme of work included developing statements that would serve as guidelines for international auditing practices, organising and conducting the future International Congresses and establishing regular communication with the exchange of technical information amongst its members. Its initial organisation and original goals are described by Chetkovich (1979) and its operating procedures and progress by Sempier (1979).

Although there was supposed to be a difference between these two bodies, their roles were seen by many people to be somewhat similar. The IASC had the responsibility of issuing international accounting standards. The IFAC was intended to be the voice of the worldwide accounting profession on all matters other than international accounting standards. The 12th International Congress held in Mexico in 1982 saw the moving closer together of the IASC and the IFAC. The two bodies agreed on a series of mutual commitments which included:

- All professional accountancy bodies making up the membership of the IFAC being automatically members of the IASC. Thus from 1 January 1984, the memberships would be identical and be drawn from 84 professional bodies, representing some 60 countries.

- The IASC will retain full autonomy in its accounting standard-setting role, and will continue to issue, in its own name, the resulting drafts and standards. It has authority to liaise with outside bodies in both the development and promulgation of those standards.

- The IFAC undertakes to support the adoption of international accounting standards by engendering the active cooperation of its professional members. Publication and acceptance of international standards will be sought in their respective countries, and pressure brought to bear on auditors governments and the business community to ensure that published financial statements comply with these standards or disclose non-compliance.

The IASC and the IFAC have their critics. "The IFAC is becoming seen by many as an organisation heavily influenced - some would say even manipulated by the North American profession". "There are signs that IFAC's appearance is increasingly viewed by Europeans and other accountants as tainted with American bias". (World Accounting Report, December 1982). In the same report the IASC is also accused of bias "despite the accepted wisdom that the British, Dutch and North Americans are streets ahead of the rest in almost all aspects of accounting". One problem is that not everyone follows the accepted wisdom! These criticisms and others will be considered in detail later in this chapter.

As well as the private sector bodies referred to above, who are interested in increasing accounting harmonization, there are also certain international public bodies interested in the financial statements of companies. These include the supranational or inter governmental bodies, such as the UN, OECD, EEC and the African Accounting Council. To some extent these bodies have also been working towards a degree of harmonization of financial statements. They are certainly seeking greater levels of disclosure by transnational companies.

In 1976 the OECD published a Code of Conduct for multinational enterprises, which was well received. Following this the sub-committee of the OECD concerned with international investment and MN enterprises set up a working group to consider accounting standards. One of the mandates of this group was to "review attempts by private bodies and international organisations to improve comparability or to achieve harmonization of accounting standards and to identify actual problem areas". The working group is not an accounting standard setting body. Nor in considering international standards will it "accord a privileged position to any one professional institution" (Zund 1983). The committee pays attention to the views on international disclosure not just of representatives of the accounting profession but also to the views of employees and endeavours to "cultivate contact with the public". The OECD working group is in fact giving priority in its deliberations to reporting by multinational enterprises and to the effective operation of the guidelines with respect to these international businesses.

Another group of specialists are working on problems of accounting and disclosure under the auspices of the UN. Whereas the OECD working group only includes specialists from industrial nations, the UN group includes experts from developing countries. The OECD group is primarily concerned with the clarification and implementation of its guidelines, the UN group is currently working on minimum disclosure requirements. Both groups are concerned indirectly with harmonization, but in both cases the priority issue is disclosure.

A problem with both bodies is that in common with many committees concerned with international issues, decisions are arrived at on the basis of consensus. The bargaining process with the UN is particularly complicated, there is a North-South division and a division between the OECD countries and the developing countries. The working groups for both bodies are intergovernmental, which means that usually delegations are composed of high level civil servants.

A member of both working parties, Professor Zund from Switzerland is pessimistic as to the outcome (1983): "The time does not yet seem to be ripe for international measures towards the harmonization of standards of accounting and reporting and endeavours in this direction may have to be carried out on a private level, for example through the IASC". He regards the fate of the OECD Working Group in a more optimistic light than that of the UN group. He points out that it is not an accounting standards setting body, it regards itself as "a forum for energising the endeavours towards the harmonization of international and national bodies". "There is a lesson to be learned from the work of both commissions: the world of accounting is extraordinarily manifold and varied, and a harmonization cannot be forced. It can only be aspired to and worked towards in a step-by-step process over the years, and it is questionable whether it will ever be achieved. But at least the first steps have now been taken" (Zund 1983).

According to the Executive Director of the Centre for Transnational Corporations"The United Nations is committed to the long term objective of establishing an international, comparable system of standardised accounting and reporting" (UN - Spring 1980). The ad hoc committee set up to achieve this objective, has set itself a number of ambitious plans, including i) the continuous development of international standards which meet current and changing needs, ii) the consultation and negotiation to secure international agreement amongst governments, iii) the promotion of standards to gain wide acceptance by interested parties such as commerce and industry, labour organisation, professional and regulating bodies as well as academic institutions and iv) the consistent application at national and international level.

Here is the ultimate blue-print for international standards, with the main supra-governmental body committed to it. Unfortunately although the ambition may be there, the methods of achieving the ambitions are far from clear. Such a programme of activities would at the best take many years to achieve and there are doubts as to whether the ultimate objective can be ever achieved.

Fitzgerald and Kelley (1979) comment that the 1977 UN Report on standards which concentrates on disclosure is only the tip of the iceberg, an initial step towards the goal of standardisation. They believe however that they have a long way to go. Pomeranz (1981) and Fitzgerald (1981) both discuss the recent activities and the roles of the UN, OECD and EEC with respect to harmonization. Fitzgerald would like to see closer and more effective cooperation between the various standard setting bodies, but does not see generally accepted worldwide accounting principles or disclosure practices "in the foreseeable future, if ever".

c) The Arguments for Harmonization

One important question that arises in connection with international standards is whether the perceived need for international accounting is genuine, and universal, or whether it is merely a partisan point of view of a number of interested parties. Zeff (1978) suggests that international standards will only be accepted when economic interest prevails. "I predict that countries such as the US, the UK, and Canada will begin to issue standards in response to what is perceived to be economic consequences. And countries that might otherwise follow these standards might find that there is no need for harmonization, and that will be the end of international standards".

Burggraaff (1980) who has been Chairman of IASC makes a similar point. He believes that international standards will be accepted not because the standards are enforced, but because industry feels that the standards are fair presentations of operations, and that it is in their own interest to use internationally accepted standards. We will now consider which interest groups would benefit from international standards. The arguments relating to the main possible beneficiaries, investors, multinational companies, large international accounting firms, regional economic groups, and developing countries are given below. Mason (1977, 1978) in presenting an excellent survey of the arguments for international standardization, identifies eleven different class of users who would benefit from such standardizations.

i) Investors

The main argument for such standards would seem to be that they are needed by those investors who wish to invest outside their own country, that is both transnational companies investing directly and individual investors wishing to invest part of a portfolio of funds. Business is increasingly becoming more international, and the argument is that it would become even more international if investors were not confused by the variety of reporting requirements and the difficulties of making comparisons.

Harmonization therefore would or could lead to improvements in the allocation of financial resources. Investors make decisions, and one source of information on which the decisions are based is the financial statement of a company. Harmonization would help to avoid confusion and possible misallocation of resources. Undoubtedly there is a problem, the difficulty faced when making comparisons has already been referred to in the previous chapter. A further problem of interpreting different accounting practices has been illustrated by Mason (1976).

The reasonableness of this argument seems very apparent to some supporters of harmonization. Sir Henry Benson, a former Chairman of IASC believes that "a degree of uniformity in accounting matters was (is) not only desirable, but necessary". (Benson 1980). He is quoted as saying "international accounting standards are much like motherhood ... a good thing" (see Burton 1980).

Cummings and Chetkovich (1978) both partners in large accounting firms, wrote "it is obvious that there is a need to harmonize accounting and reporting standards". The authors are concerned at the differences in accounting practices throughout the world. They recognise that it "may not always be possible to achieve universal acceptance of a single method of accounting and reporting ... the fact is that the promulgation of an international standard reduces the alternatives available under varying circumstances and that the required disclosures facilitate understanding and comparison". Lafferty (1980) points to the difficulty that he and other journalists face in reporting financial results to readers who may be investors in companies in several different countries.

Carey (1970) in making a case for uniform international standards argues, "Private capital cannot flow freely over international boundaries unless the investors can receive reliable information about what is being done with their money and this means financial statements audited by accountants in whom the investors have confidence". It is difficult to argue that private capital cannot flow freely without this condition being met. Private capital has flowed freely for a number of centuries. Investors are interested in balancing returns with risks. It is true that unreliable information adds to the risk, but if the expected returns are high enough the funds will still flow.

Most (1964) and others have argued that financial statements published in Europe are, in fact, comparable with those published in the United States. Based upon the figures given in their financial statements, it is possible to ascertain the strengths and weaknesses of companies in different countries and their relative profit performance. Most alleges that an investor should be able to rank the companies "... in order of preference for investment purposes by relating the operating results data to the conclusions drawn about structure". He is arguing that a good investment analyst is able to make the necessary adjustments to enable statements to be comparable. "Accounts are approximations, and there is no reason to believe that distortions arising from national differences of accounting practice, company legislation or business ethics are of greater weight than those distortions which may arise from a wide variety of other causes".

It cannot be denied that international harmonization would make comparisons easier, with not so many adjustments being required. But international investment has and still does go on without standardisation. It has in fact not been shown that the variety of systems really act as a restraint on international investment and international business.

ii) Multinational Companies

Multinational companies would benefit from harmonization for the following reasons:

a) Consolidation of overseas subsidiaries would be easier if accounting practices were standardized.

b) Many large companies want to raise money in more than one country and in international markets, and so need to produce accounts which can easily be understood by investors in many countries. For this reason the World Federation of Stock Exchanges is said to be encouraging the acceptance of international accounting standards (Thomas 1975).

c) It would be easier, and possibly greater accuracy could be obtained, in valuing and appraising overseas companies for merger purposes.

d) Management control would be easier.

Morgan (1967) expressed the views of many multinational businessmen when he wrote

> Communications improvements, aiding the understanding of ideas of others, is the big need because we do not really understand each others backgrounds, cultures and languages. Accounting principles are another area of concern to multi-national companies. As a United States Corporation whose shareholders are mainly United States citizens or financial institutions, we feel a strong responsibility for issuing a set of financial statements which are meaningful in US terms. Consider, however that host countries legally require accounts in forms that do not differ from local tax rules.

The article is an appeal for international standards or at least for making life easier for international businessmen.

Choi (1973) suggests that corporations will be motivated to upgrade their financial disclosure in order to appeal to investors in the international new issues market. He points out that the disclosure of information is even more important in an international setting where investors are unacquainted with the relative merits of foreign borrowers. He finds support for the hypothesis that the improvement in dislcosure of companies borrowing in the Euromerkets is greater than in those companies not borrowing in that market. The 64 firms examined who borrowed in the Euromarket significantly improved their financial disclosure upon entry into the market.

Previts (1975) reflects this common line of thinking on the subject. He believes that the central issue in international accounting is achieving uniformity of accounting principles. He sees this as the main issue because of the increasing importance of international business, and the increasing flow of funds between countries. (See also Kanaga 1980.)

Companies now often obtain listings on more than one Stock Exchange, and have to satisfy the listing requirements of each of these Exchanges. They would clearly benefit from some degree of harmonisation; the listing requirements being at present largely based on the accounting practices of the individual country. Philips, for example, reports according to one set of accounting principles in the Netherlands and according to a different set of principles in the USA. This point is returned to in the chapter on accounting problems in multinational business.

Another way in which international pressures leads to change is described by Niehus (1970). He gives details of how increasing international integration of business has made itself felt in Germany. One example being that it has become an advantage for German auditing and accounting firms to be able to point to written rules that they follow so that the international clients will better be able to understand the work that is being done. This is one reason why there have been attempts in Germany to codify certain standards for the professional performance of audits.

iii) Large International Accounting Firms

Hauworth (1973) a partner in Arthur Andersen wrote "My firm ... believes that the need for worldwide accounting standards is so great that progress in developing them should not be delayed by waiting for the creation of some authoritative international organisation". Hauworth recognises that because of the various problems in the way of obtaining acceptance of worldwide standards, it may not be possible at once to move to the widespread adoption. But such "proper worldwide accounting standards consistent with our (Arthur Andersen) views on the objectives of financial statements and our understanding of the basic economic facts underlying business transactions could be used as a platform in assisting local accounting professions in developing standards, and hopefully in breaking down resistance to the ideas". Arthur Andersen published in 1974, a book which set forth their views on what accounting standards should be for business enterprises throughout the world.

McComb (1981) points out that "the thrust of the movement towards the harmonization of accounting standards on the international level has come mainly from accountants in public practice rather than academic accountants". It could be that one of their reasons for wanting international standards is altruistic. It would make life very much easier for them if similar practices existed throughout the world. "A majority of the clients of the large Anglo-American accountancy firms have at least one foreign subsidiary or branch". "The preparation, consolidation and auditing of these companies' financial statements would become less onerous if accounting practices were standardised" (Nobes and Parker 1981). The international accounting firms would also like to be able to quote international accounting standards to clients, to give them backing for recommending certain ways of reporting. Lack of adequate control in many developing countries makes life difficult for auditors of parent companies that have subsidiaries in such countries. (See Tipgos 1981.)

The international accounting firms are worried generally about the increasing interest of outsiders in the profession. They wish the standard setting process to be kept out of the hands of the government. At an Arthur Young Conference, when disussing the future of international accounting, Kanaga (1980), expresses the belief that the role of outsiders in the accounting process will increase. As one example of this he mentions the needs of the third world, who through its "clout in the UN" will be seeking more financial information on transnational business. He sees the role of national and international governmental bodies increasing. He does not welcome this trend. As to the future of the accounting firms, he sees a growing number of international alliances between strong professional firms, and is optimistic about auditing standards becoming more uniform around the world. He is hopeful that IASC will be successful in their work, preferring them to adopt a middle ground on standards; that is one of allowing some flexibility of practice but certainly eliminating obvious bad practice. If the IASC fails in its work, he believes that the UN or regional governmental bodies will move in to try to obtain greater disclosure and more consistent practice.

At the same 1980 Roundtable Conference, Macrae, also of Arthur Young, discussed the difficulties of the international accounting firms. He points to the fact that in many countries local accounting firms are growing up, and they resent the strong influence of the international accounting firms in their country. He believes that it is unfortunate that nationalism has become an impediment to a free international market in accounting.

The interesting point is made that much of the increasing nationalism in the profession, "results from local reactions to the attitude of some expatriate accountants that what is right for their country is right for everyone else. I have found that many American and British expatriate accountants still persist in this attitude. It seems clear to me that the French and South American developments ... are based to a substantial degree on the insensitivity of the expatriate accountant to his local colleagues' needs and opinions".

The nationalism referred to resulted in 1976, in foreign accounting firms practising in France being required to conform to French standards including registration with the French professional society. A new rule on qualifications for foreign accountants wishing to practice in France, required them to sit an oral examination.

The EEC could also introduce rules which could be a hindrance to the practice at an international level of accounting firms. The first draft of the Eighth Directive proposed restraining the ability of non-EEC qualified accountants to operate in EEC member countries. There were also proposals that non-EEC qualified accountants could not hold the majority of the capital of EEC accounting firms. These were only proposals and the directive has been amended, but they reveal the extent of regional feeling.

Seidler (1969) had referred to nationalism interfering with the transfer of international skills. He refers to how historically "the most effective vehicle for the international transfer of accounting skills has been the international accounting firms". He makes reference to how with the continued international expansion of American corporations and the resulting demand for services from the international accounting firms "it might be expected that this international transfer would continue". He regards it as unfortunate that "the international expansion of the Anglo-American based international accounting firms appears to be generating a reaction in a number of countries". He mentions however that the USA is one of the countries that restricts the right of foreigners to practise.

Seidler's argument, referring to the continual expansion of Anglo-American based accounting firms is exactly the sort of argument that would frighten national accounting firms in both developed and less developed countries. He believes that the restriction on many types of foreign business may be justified in a country on the grounds that, with say mining, it limits the exploitation or expropriation of the national wealth. But with accounting he sees the possibilities of such exploitation of national wealth as virtually nil. In fact the restrictions he believes reduce efficiency, and just provide benefits to one group of the country's population namely the local practising accountants.

Seidler is arguing for free markets, based on the theory that these produce maximum economic performance. Fortunately or unfortunately governments make decisions on political grounds as well as economic. The development of a local accounting profession, with ownership and decision making in local hands is a reasonable political goal even if it is at an economic cost. Some degree of nationalism is understandable, and as Seidler points out the international firm can on occasions be said to have helped bring about the political pressures it faces by insensitivity to local needs.

iv) Regional Economic Groups

Large regional economic communities have been created in recent years, and these usually have as one of their objectives, the promotion of trade within their region. In order to improve understanding and working relationships within the region, harmonization over a wide number of topics needs to take place. There are therefore official attempts at harmonizing commercial law and accounting within these communities. The activities of such regional groups will be considered at the end of this chapter.

v) Developing Countries

There is an argument that countries that do not have any domestic accounting standards would benefit from international standards in that it would enable them to adopt a ready made system. They would not have to produce their own, they could adopt (perhaps with some slight modification) the international standards. If this were possible it would of course save them a great deal of time and expense.

Benson (1975) has made reference to the fact that "a number of relatively small nations are crying out for international standards". Many developing nations do take a great interest in international standards. Nigeria, for example, one of the developing countries who are members of the IASC, have adopted these standards and companies over a certain size are required to produce accounts that conform to such standards. The subject of international standards and developing countries will be returned to later in the book.

vi) Other Interest Groups

One group who it is said would benefit from a greater degree of harmonization would be Tax Authorities. They would find their work less complicated when dealing with foreign income. It must be remembered however that it is taxation rules that are responsible for many of the differences that do exist in accounting practices. Tax is and will remain a national matter. Accounting measurement may be harmonized, but it would need to be recognised that standardised accounting practices may need to be adjusted for national tax purposes.

Other user groups who could benefit from harmonization include International Credit agencies and labour unions.

d) Who Should Set and Enforce International Standards?

i) The profession or governmental bodies?

One crucial question that has to be considered by those who want international standards, is who should set these standards? Can international accounting standards be established by a voluntary effort on the part of the profession or must they be established within a context - either organisational or governmental - that has the capability to enforce them?

There is a strong belief within the profession worldwide, that they should set accounting standards. Arguments to support this view include the fact that it is professional accountants who are experts on the subject. They have a thorough knowledge of business environment and business practices, and of the accounting treatments that are appropriate to reflect the business situation. Professional accountants are independent from both preparers (management) and users (investors). They can express an unbiased opinion on how transactions, events and conditions can be best accounted for in order to ensure that financial statements fairly present the financial position and results. (See Burggraaff 1982.)

But the user groups are not always inclined to accept the opinion of the so called unbiased experts. And the less so in a case where it appears that such opinion is not purely based on hard fact or iron logic, but in part on judgement. The measurement of a company's profit involves judgement. The validity of that judgement can be questioned by anybody who feels his interests have been affected adversely. Interest groups are biased, and they have a right to make their own value judgements which will be influenced by their interests. They have every right to question the profession's judgement as to whether or not proper consideration has been given to all interests affected.

Partly to overcome this problem, the IASC decided in 1981 to set up a new consultative group to increase the involvement of the user community and other non-accountants in the standard setting process. They were recognising that to improve the acceptability of their standards, it was necessary to obtain wider involvement. In fact they encountered difficulty in obtaining increased participation.

Kraayenhof (1960) supports the view that standards should be set by the profession. "For all countries basing their economic structure on free enterprise" the choice of uniform accounting principles should not be kept in the hands of the government. He supports the view of Eaton (1957) "it would probably mean the end of progress".

There are attempts to increase the credibility of international accounting standards. Kirkpatrick (1981) believes that the international audit firms should do more to help with harmonization. "The international companies are now being encouraged to acknowledge in their annual reports that in conforming to national accounting standards they also report in conformity in all material respects, with international standards. There would be a great logic in the international audit firms stating publicly that they support the adoption of the IASC's standards wherever possible (i.e. where the law permits) worldwide".

The profession clearly wishes to back IASC. There are those (Sycip 1981) who believe that the UN should recognise IASC as the body most qualified to set up international standards. The UN should then use its authority to hasten universal acceptance of such international standards.

As mentioned the IASC has tried to increase its acceptability. Representatives of Stock Exchanges, Labour Unions and Financial Analysts were invited to join. Almost all the organisations asked refused the invitation. Burggraaff (1982) who at the time was retiring chairman of IASC regarded such refusals as 'something of a surprise', but explains that the reasons for the rejections were that

a) some user groups under their own constitutions are unable to give a mandate to support international standards, which was a precondition for membership of the committee.

b) others have inadequate secretariats.

c) others have inadequate financial resources.

d) and some could not give high priority to IAS, as they had problems of their own to settle.

Burggraaff in the 1982 interview defended the work of the IASC; he did not believe that the statements produced had been too flexible and did not see as a threat in the immediate future the work on disclosure of the UN or OECD. As he explained these two bodies were mainly concerned with disclosures, and not the regulation of measurement practice. The IASC are particularly concerned with measurement. He believed that within the next five years (to 1987) there would have been big developments with IASC.

As at the end of 1983 IASC had largely failed to get companies throughout the world to refer to its standards in their annual reports. However in Canada companies must make reference to international standards, as must listed companies in Italy. Burggraaff reports that in Denmark, and possibly soon also in Norway and Italy, there has been a move away from tax based accounts, and the IASC could claim some credit for this. Burggraaff (1982) would like to see multinational companies complying with international standards and stating that they were doing so.

Mueller (1981) gives three major reasons why the IASC may be viewed as an ineffective and inappropriate agency for setting international standards. First, there is the potential conflict between the standards set by IASC and those set by the national bodies. Second, in many countries accounting standards need to be incorporated in law and set by political procedures. Third, there is no political and diplomatic recognition of IASC by national governments or international agreements. The IASC does however participate in the discussion on standards by the appropriate UN and OECD groups.

McComb (1982) draws attention to the different objectives of the public and private bodies. He sees the EEC harmonization programme as having a macroeconomic slant and the impetus to the programme being to improve regional coordination by reducing differences in commercial law and accounting practices. The factors that gave impetus to the formation of the IASC are seen to be the increasing internationalism of business, the growth of international capital markets, and the increasing international involvement of the accounting profession. McComb sees problems with cooperation between the public and private standard setting bodies, because of this "conflict of disparate objectives".

It is argued by some that there is no need for any standards to be set and enforced, neither national nor international. They argue that the level of disclosure should be left to market pressure to determine. If the managers of a company see it as in the interest of the company to respond to the information demands of users, then managements will produce the information. If users are not satisfied with the amount of information a company discloses then they can leave that company alone. An argument against this is that the bargaining strength of the company may differ from that of the user. Clearly the UN, the OECD and the EEC do not believe that market forces can be relied upon to produce relevant and comparable data. For a discussion on this issue see Gray, Shaw and McSweeney (1981).

Jaggi (1973) makes the point that the results of his analysis indicate that as a result of managerial value orientations the reliability of financial statements in developing countries is likely to be low. He believes that if the disclosure of information in these countries is left to individual firms there appears only a small probability that the reliabiality can be improved. He sees the governments in developing countries as being important in developing principles and providing legal authority. This it is believed, will lead to higher realiability of financial disclosure. He is emphasising that it will not be sufficient to leave it to the profession nor to the firms.

The problem of who should set international standards can be seen to be complex. Standards for companies based within a country (whether or not they have foreign interests) can be settled either by the profession within that country or by the government of the country. These national standards can be enforced. But who can enforce international standards? If the government of a particular country adopts an international standard to be applied within that country it can enforce that standard. The position of multinational companies is however more complicated. It could be argued that it is up to the government of any country in which an MNC invests to demand and obtain the information it needs. Often, however, the government is in a weak bargaining position when it comes to dealing with the MNC. The case is often made therefore for supranational bodies to set such international standards and to force companies to comply with the reporting needs.

Developing countries are anxious to seek foreign capital, they are anxious to attract foreign investment. They are in a weak bargaining position, particularly because they are in competition with other developing countries to attract these funds. If one country allows MNC to get away with low levels of disclosure, there is pressure on others to do the same. Therefore it can be argued it is only if a supranational body such as the UN, enforces equal standards on all, that international standards of reporting can be raised.

The setting of international standards, particularly in the extent to which they apply to MNC's is a political process (Gray, Shaw, McSweeney 1981). If this is accepted then it follows that it is intergovernmental bodies that are more likely to achieve success with the setting and enforcing of international standards. The accounting profession can play a supportive role, and will certainly be needed to provide assistance.

If a national government adopts a standard, perhaps developed by the profession, then the government can enforce it on all companies that operate within that country. If the government does not adopt the standard, the profession have only limited means of ensuring that companies, particularly large MNCs adopt the standard.

The same criticism can however be made of international standards produced by such supra-national bodies as the UN and OECD. If national governments do not wish to enforce these standards within their country, then there are few sanctions the UN and OECD can adopt in order to obtain compliance. These bodies can produce 'guidelines'. But it is difficult to see them as anything other than guidelines, "because compliance can be enforced only at the national level or in regional grouping equivalent to the national level such as the EEC". (Gray et al 1981).

This is the path the EEC seems to be taking. In October 1981 the European Parliament adopted a report calling for greater control of multinational enterprises. The disclosure requirements covered in the report are very similar to those incorporated in the OECD guidelines. One has, therefore, a supranational body making proposals, these proposals are later adopted by a regional governmental body that has the power to make arrangements and enforce them.

The pressures for increased MNC accountability have led not only to demands for increasing disclosure, but also for some degree of international harmonization, for some international standards. The proposals on this subject are designed mainly to apply to MNCs. In the UN proposals (1977) the emphasis is on all large MNC's, but application to uninational companies is also recommended. The OECD proposals (1976) refer to all MNC's but they would also like uninational firms to adopt them. If the proposals of these two bodies were adopted it could lead to dual standards, MNCshaving to report in one way, to meet international demands, and all companies incorporated within a country, whether owning foreign subsidiaries or not, reporting in another way to satisfy the national demands of the home country. It is also possible that a MNC may have to report in a third way, namely to meet the demands of the host country. It being possible that neither the home country nor the host country would be satisfied with the requirements of the supranational intergovernmental agencies.

EEC proposals are intended to apply to all companies that have activities within the EEC. IAS proposals are also intended to apply to all companies whether or not they are multinational. "What is likely to develop is blocs of accounting uniformity" within economic groupings. (Arpan and Radebaugh, 1981).

There are numerous proposals for multiple accounting reports. With some companies having to report according to one set of standards to satisfy domestic requirements and according to another set of standards for its international business. Wilkinson (1963) argued in the first edition of the International Journal that the "best we can expect is that each country will recognise the other countries' justification for its principles". This would mean that one must accept the idea "that one company can put out more than one set of financial statements". This point will be returned to later in the chapter.

ii) The Basis for International Standards

A fundamental problem in accounting standard setting, whether at the national or international level, is on what basis the decision is made to adopt one practice and to reject another. There are two possible approaches, one would be to agree on a conceptual framework, to agree on what was wanted from an accounting system and then to see which of the alternatives came nearest to satisfying the objectives. The alternative is to arrive at a committee decision, at a consensus, where the committee is made up of a number of knowledgable people, with or without vested interests, and subject to political lobbying.

In practice it is the second of these two alternatives that is followed. It has become accepted that accounting standards and regulations must be seen as a political process. Watts and Zimmerman (1978) have shown how lobbying can affect particular accounting standards. Their research relates to the USA but there is no reason to believe that it does not equally apply to international standards. Watts and Zimmerman report that a former chairman of the FASB complained of political lobbying. A former chairman of IASC also complained "As long as financial accounting standards have potential effects on the firms future cashflows, standard setting by bodies, such as... will be met by corporate lobbying" (Burggraaff 1982). We could include any standard setting body in this sentence, that is any body that hoped in a democratic situation to have its standards adopted.

Standard makers, whether national or international have to bow to political pressures. This point has been well argued by Solomons (1978). Zeff (1978) points out that lobbying (in the USA) has existed in accounting for well over 40 years. Zeff illustrates in some detail how since the 1940's various groups have invested a great deal of effort in lobbying for or against various accounting pronouncements. Horngren (1981) states "The (FASB) engages in policy making, which may be defined as the process by which individuals or groups in power choose general rules for action that may affect others within an organisation or perhaps an entire society".

Horngren, Zeff and Solomons were referring to problems of domestic standard setting but the same applies to international standards, where in fact the problems are greater as there is less unity of purpose and more disparate goals than at a national level. As Boritz (1982) mentions "there is a growing belief that accounting may be far more than the innocuous practice so many people feel it to be. Accounting is being touted as a social choice mechanism". Accounting information has value - there are economic consequences associated with changes in accounting rules. "Agreement, compromise and political forces, rather than undisputable laws determine which standards ought to be adopted". (Boritz 1982).

Kirk (1981) who was chairman of the FASB at the time of writing, discusses the role of consensus versus concepts in standard setting. He argued that "the notion that financial reporting standards redistribute wealth is exaggerated". He was not arguing that it had no effect, just that the effect was exaggerated. He was also talking about the position in the USA. If we move from the USA to countries where there is less control over the distribution of information, where there are not S.E.C.s then the effect on redistribution would be expected to be greater.

The whole of standard setting, national as well as international is a political process. The move to standards was the result of criticism of the existing form of financial reporting and as a result of pressure, accounting standards committees were created.

Laughlin and Puxty (1982) differentiate between accounting rules and standards being based on group or party interests and being based on groups' or parties' concepts of a 'worldview'. Watts and Zimmerman (1979) and Hope (1979) see a number of groups involved in the standard setting process, each group having a set of interests. The interests being based in particular on self regard in such matters as wealth transfer. Laughlin and Puxty prefer to see the debate over regulations and standards as being based on differences in the worldview of the groups. Worldview being "the opinions, theories and attitudes formed within a class in order to defend and promote its interests". Within a group there are common views based not so much on material gain but rather in terms of affiliation to certain values.

Burggraaff (1983) discusses the political pressures on IASC. He differentiates between political pressure coming from various interest groups in the private sector and political pressure from government bodies, and government agencies who are interested in international standards. The pressure that the various interest groups from time to time bring on the IASC, places the committee in an uncomfortable dilemma. The pressure means that the committees decision making process either has to be based on consensus and compromise or on resorting to underlying concepts.

The consensus approach involves seeking the views of the various interest groups. "When pursuing this road, standard setting takes on some of the characteristics of the legislative process in a democratic society. Every party may have its own far reaching objectives in mind, guiding their preference . But it is not those objectives that are up for debate, but only the practical implications for a certain subject. By this process political pressures are not eliminated, but canalised. Having heard the debate, standard setters have to decide what solution would gain sufficient support. There should be some sort of consensus, that more often than not leads to a compromise: nobody is quite satisfied, but most parties are prepared to settle for it just now, waiting for the next opportunity in future".

In this process, there is one important constraint: no standard should violate the well considered and firm conviction of the profession as to what constitutes proper accounting. Accounting standard setting may have political implications, but basically the exercise is, or should be, a technical exercise. Burggraaff believes that nothing good will be achieved if the value judgements of the unbiased experts are replaced by the value judgements of the biased interest groups.

Burggraaff(1983) wishes Governments to confine their role in accounting standard setting to fundamentals. He recognises that in society information means power, and governments cannot afford to leave this power outside their control. However he believes legislation is not the ideal role for setting accounting standards. This is particularly true he feels at the international level. Standards are needed at an international level because an enterprise can now affect the lives of people in more than one country. Interest groups wish to have access to relevant information. He would prefer to see the inter-governmental bodies restricting themselves to broad issues, and to leave details on such issues as profit measurement to IASC. He believes that standard setters whether national or international should recognise that no standard will be effective unless it has sufficient support in the community and in the profession. It should also be recognised that no support from the community will be forthcoming unless a standard strikes a fair balance between conflicting interests; and that no support from the profession will be forthcoming, unless a standard improves truth and fairness of presentation, as perceived by the profession.

Walker (1978) suggests that IASC may be a paper tiger, and if this is correct then it "would be of little interest to potential lobbyists". In fact his research shows that the IASC were subject to political lobbying, and so presumably is not a paper tiger. He examines the international standard on 'Consolidated Financial Statements' that was published in 1976, the exposure draft and research which preceded the statement, and the rules and practices in various countries relating to consolidated statements and the use of equity accounting. He sees his work as a case study of how the IASC obtains agreement on accounting standards. He concludes "it appears that the IASC wanted to accommodate every view, regardless of whether those views were consistent or not with a particular analytical framework". He further concludes that "the process used to achieve agreement on IAS 3 suggests that the IASC is not meeting its stated objective of formulating and publishing 'basic standards' or of concentrating on 'essentials'. 'Agreement' on procedures in IAS 3 was accomplished by ignoring the conflict between the rationale underlying this or that national standard. Instead, the IASC catalogues those technical procedures on which representatives of different national accounting bodies could agree. This plan of action may seem to be diplomatic. It may encourage the view that progress is being made in resolving disputes in accounting. But it may also have deleterious effects. The rules which emerge may add to the difficulty of unravelling inconsistent lines of argument about the aims of specific accounting techniques - and hence foster confusion in the practice of accounting in different countries".

Gerboth (1973) borrowed from the literature on policy-making to suggest that the APB's process of formulating accounting standards could be looked upon as a rational and useful task of 'muddling through'. One wonders whether the IASC could be said to be 'muddling through'.

How easy is it to arrive at a consensus? Stamp (1982) attempted to reach a consensus amongst accountants on what they considered the most important concepts, that should lie behind accounting standards. He was trying to construct a logical algebra of rights, duties, privileges and the like. This was an interesting approach; it was recognising that it is unlikely we will ever arrive at conceptual framework based on theory.

A problem arises however, in that whereas a group of accountants may be able to reach consensus this is not necessarily what other members of society would have agreed to be the correct order of importance. Accounts are prepared not just to satisfy accountants but also users' needs. How are views of users going to be brought into this ranking. It is alright for the profession to agree on the order of priorities but is this the same order of priorities as the rest of the society would produce. If we wish to have accounting backed by the rule of law then standards which are acceptable to society would need to be introduced. The law cannot enforce ideas which although acceptable to accountants are those that would be against the wishes of the rest of society.

Stamp's scheme is a way of resolving conflicts in accounting. However, the way in which it is resolved depends upon the people who are asked and in an international context upon the country in which the questions are being asked. Also who speaks for the public interest in the matter of accounting standards? The order of priorities that would be obtained could be expected to vary from country to country depending on the economic and social system in that country.

One possible solution is multiple-base reporting. As different groups and/or different countries want their financial statements prepared under different bases, the statements could show the outcome under each of these bases. This could be achieved by way of footnotes, or by supplementary statements, or by multicolumn-reporting. Under this approach political pressures are not canalised or eliminated, but are complied with by serving different groups in accordance with their demands.

Burggraaff (1982) believes that for sophisticated users this type of reporting may have merits, but for the general public it is confusing. "The ordinary reader is at a loss to determine what figure is relevant to him, and his confidence in the ability of the profession to prepare relevant and reliable figures will be eroded. Therefore, multiple-base reporting should not be adopted except in a transitional or experimental stage".

Stamp (1972) does not believe in a goal of uniformity in the sense of developing a rigid code of rules and regulations. The profession will not serve the public intent if it confines its practitioners within a straight jacket. He believes that "the wide diversity of users makes it necessary to supply information developed on different bases". The differences between countries are so great that he does not believe that with the present knowledge "universal accounting standards can possibly be developed except at a ridiculous level of generalisation".

As Burggraaff sees the problem, the only alternative to consensus is to rely on basic underlying accounting concepts. This involves some ideas in the back of the standard setters minds as to what constitutes truth and fairness in accounting. Unfortunately despite a large amount of effort, nobody has yet produced an agreed conceptual framework for accounting. There are a wide variety of objectives in accounting.

Burggraaff makes the point that "an agreed conceptual framework requires a common ideological foundation". Such a foundation does not appear to exist and so the IASC is forced back, together with the UN and OECD (and possibly the national accounting standard setting bodies) to consensus decision making.

The components of a conceptual framework are:

a) general agreement on the overall objectives of financial reporting;

b) general agreement as to the nature and needs of the various groups of users of financial reports;

c) identification of a set of criteria to be used in choosing between alternative solutions to standard setting problems.

Stamp (1982) in listing these elements is referring to a national standard setting body, but the same components would apply to a framework for international standards.

McComb (1979) argues that before we can harmonise we need more research to ascertain why the differences arise and to determine what will be the economic effects of some countries changing practices. He believes that we should study the reasons for the continuing existences of national differences in accounting principles and practices. "In that context, emphasis should be upon investigation, analysis and education rather than upon speeding the process of promulgating further international accounting standards". He is not against the idea of harmonising accounting principles and standards and believes there is a strong case for doing so. He believes, however, that this can only be achieved if there is mutual international understanding "both of corporate objectives and the rankings attached to them".

Boritz (1982) makes a similar plea for more research. He believes that empirical work should be undertaken to guide the standard setting body: "The research results of various studies of economic effects of market reaction to pronouncements can provide feedback to policy makers which will assist them in their deliberations".

The widely divergent philosophical differences between the views of the UK and USA on the one side and the Continental European countries on the other hand over the nature of the corporation in society, the way it is to be governed and who is responsible for the governing, are seen as major difficultures in the development of harmonized standards.

There are many implications for accounting research that arise from these difficulties. We have data to compare accounting practices between countries, but we lack relevant socio/political data which would enable us to interpret the difference between such practices. Given that the purpose of accounting standards is to assist the user, we need to understand that information only acquires a value when it informs: this means we must study information as a function not only of the data reported but of the user and his organisational context. Unfortunately this approach is difficult, particularly at an international level. There is likely to be wide disagreement between accountants in different countries as to which groups of users are primary constituents and which groups needs are less important.

Chambers (1972) in fact suggested a framework, which he believes would be helpful for accounting standard setting in an international community. He describes the concept of continuously contemporary accounting and suggests that adoption of this idea would overcome present difficulties of international differences in accounting practice and increase the reliability of inter-firm and international comparisons.

Chambers gives reaons why there are differences and suggests that the greatest single reason is taxation. He also suggests a new system - which would provide factual information needed by all users, i.e. managers, investors, creditors. He believes the system proposed would "provide a more reliable foundation for private negotiation and public policy than the divergent models of accounting now in use".

AlHashim and Garner (1973) also adopting a normative approach suggest a framework in which accounting might be structured uniformly in terms of its postulates, yet be able to vary its standards according to the environmental circumstances of a country. They believe that such an approach would be desirable and also acceptable.

The literature clearly indicates that international standards are at the moment being based more on consensus decision making than on satisfying objective criteria. This is inevitable as, in the absence of an agreed set of objectives for accounting and the absence of agreed criteria for choosing between alternatives, both at a national and international level, one has to rely on decisions by committees.

Baxter (1981) concludes "standards have probably led to many improvements. So long as they are bland and avoid sensitive areas, they are popular. If however, they threaten to plunge the accountant into ill-understood complexities, or to slash the profit figures of business, they are attacked and sometimes defeated". This applies equally to international standards. IASC are now producing standards and exposure drafts on the more controversial aspects of the subject; it can be expected therefore that either the criticism will mount, or that non-compliance with the standards will increase.

Stamp (1972) believes that we should promote greater international cooperation in the fields of accounting, including work on international standards. Any such standards must be based, however, on a coherent and logical theoretical structure, which at the moment does not exist. Without such a basis standards must be arbitrary. Therefore whatever standards are developed, should not be rigidly enforced.

iii) Compliance with International Standards

The majority of accountants appear to support self regulation; they are not in favour of governmental control (see Benson 1976 and 1980). The rules of the profession being less objectionable than the rules of the government. A number of other parties are however interested in international standards, such as companies, employees, tax authorities and they might not agree on regulation by the accounting profession. They would still be submitting to an external authority, and would prefer an enforcing agency in which they felt they had influence.

When IASC was founded in 1973, the members agreed to use their best endeavours to ensure that published financial statements would comply with the forthcoming international standards. They in effect hoped that accountants would take into account compliance with international standards (in addition to local standards) when granting audit certificates. "The IASC's objectives were widely supported in professional journals in several countries" (Walker 1978). As Walker points out, however, the reality was different. The levels of support given when it came to obtaining compliance varied from country to country. In the USA the international standards only had to be followed if the FASB adopted them. In the UK, the international standards were expected to be followed when they did not conflict with UK standards. Similarly in Australia international standards only had to be followed when they did not conflict with local standards.

In 1978 the IASC published revised wordings relating to the agreement of members, acknowledging that IASC pronouncements would not override local regulations. IASC's task was to be one of attempting to bring about changes in existing national standards so that they fitted in with what were seen to be agreed essentials. Members were now to try to influence national standards, rather than to use their best endeavours to ensure companies complied with IAS. The major influence of members of the IASC it was hoped would be on the standard setting committees in member countries.

Evans and Taylor (1982) point out that the IASC has no real authority to implement its recommendations "and must rely on the best efforts of individual members which most often are not the accounting standard setting bodies of these countries". Choi and Bavishi (1982) also worried by this lack of compliance suggested the IASC should concentrate its attention on the areas of accounting where major differences between countries do exist. The research of Choi and Bavishi indicates that in the 24 countries they studied, fundamental differences in accounting standards are "not as extensive as one would expect". The IASC (1975) believed that it would be five to ten years before the full effects of its actions would be recognised. The studies on the level of compliance with IASC standards do not indicate that this prediction will be achieved.

Choi and Bavishi would like to see the IASC take on more of a leadership role, and concentrate their attention on topics where standardisation is most urgent. They saw the work of the IASC up to the time of writing their paper as being one "of maintaining the status quo", of concentrating on areas where there are not major differences. Some of the topics that have recently been tackled by the IASC would however seem to be attempting to do more than maintain the status quo. Standards on leasing and the capitalisation of interest were produced by the IASC before the UK Accounting Standards Committee.

The IASC has not received much international support for its pronouncements. This point has been made by the UN (1982) and others. Evans and Taylor (1982) in a study to determine the impact of IASC standards on the financial reporting in member nations, conclude that the standards had had little impact on companies annual reports up to the end of 1980. "Except for a few instances, a country following a particular method prior to the promulgation of an IASC standard continued to follow the same principle after the standard issuance".

Mason (1981) in an examination of the annual reports of the companies in the Fortune List of the top 500 corporations in the USA between 1978 and June 1980 found "no reference whatever to the IASC or its pronouncements". Lafferty et al (1979) in a study of the accounts of the 100 major European Companies found that reference to IASC standards are "few and far between".

In Canada where according to Thomas (1977) the professional body strongly supports international accounting standards and where the profession say it is desirable to disclose conformity with or deviations from such standards the 1979 survey of the largest Canadian companies accounts by the Canadian Institute of Chartered Accountants found that none had in fact mentioned compliance. Perhaps however the position has changed since 1979. It was reported in 1983 that a "number of Canadian corporations" were referring to adherence to international standards in their annual report (Elliott 1983). Monitoring compliance with international accounting standards is now becoming an important area for research.

But what does compliance mean? The fact that a company does not mention the international accounting standard in its annual report does not mean the accounts have not been prepared according to such standards. Researchers can just as easily make mistakes the other way. The fact that a national standard is changed and the change means that it results in a similar approach to a problem as that of the international standard, does not mean that the national body made the change to conform to the international standard. Evans and Taylor (1982) imply that the UK standard on the valuation and presentation of inventories was changed "to conform to IASC No. 2". Causation is a very hard thing to prove and certainly involves the use of more advanced research methods than have so far been used in international accounting research.

Nair and Frank (1981) detected in their research that countries were moving closer together in their accounting practices. They examined 131 accounting practices common to the 1973, 1975 and 1979 Price Waterhouse surveys of accounting practices, and found greater agreement between countries in practices in the later surveys than in the earlier. They recognise that inference of causation is not an easy task, but do state that "the period of the IASC's existence has coincided with a growing harmonization of accounting standards". They are not able to say that the IASC has been responsible for this, but do say that the association between IAS and increased harmonization "is strengthened by the fact that many of the topics on which the IASC has issued pronouncements are those on which the authors observe harmonization".

The IASC have indicated that they plan (from 1982) to pay more attention to ensuring compliance with the standards that have already been issued than to preparing new standards (World Accounting Report December 1982). The Chairman of the IASC commented that it would be a great achievement if at the next International Congress "the majority of member countries enterprises engaged in international trade or share dealings acknowledged compliance with both local and international accounting standards". (Elliott 1983).

Clearly compliance and the role of the IASC is a topical issue. As Thomas (1980) commented the real difficulty of the IASC lies in achieving implementation, and he believes that to achieve this it is necessary to obtain governmental help.

Mason (1978) in his very thorough analysis of the problems of international standards lists 13 difficulties in the way of achieving standardisation including enforcement problems, the indifference or opposition of most accountants if not their professional bodies, and the reluctance of many national bodies to take the required action. Mason obtained information on the financial reporting standards of many countries and then carried out an in depth analysis of certain countries. His object was to identify common features which might be helpful to standardisation, and to identify those aspects and problems which might prevent standardisation. His conclusion was somewhat pessimistic; he did not see international financial reporting standards being established in the near future. There is of course an alternative to enforcement, namely voluntary compliance. Choi (1974) suggests that those companies that wish to raise money through the international financial markets will voluntarily improve their disclosure. This may be a more useful and better way of improving disclosure than the mandatory requirements.

e) Arguments Against Harmonization Leading to International Standards

Already in this section a number of obstacles that stand in the way of international standards have been mentioned. These difficulties, and the argument against such standardisation will now be considered more fully. The arguments against can be summarised as coming under one or more of the following headings:

i) There are cultural differences between countries, which means that the objectives of the accounting system can differ from country to country.

ii) It is necessary to agree on the objectives at the national level before it is possible to move to international standards.

iii) The process is very complicated and expensive, and so not worth the effort.

iv) Nationalism stands in the way of change.

v) If harmonization is achieved it will be by the acceptance of the lowest acceptable level of reporting.

vi) Needs of developing countries differ from those of the developed.

Fantl (1971) argues that "one of the chief and least recognised misconceptions which occurs in international accounting is the assumption that accounting objectives are uniform". Fantl's point is that if we are going to achieve harmonization, we can only do so when all countries have the same objectives from their accounting systems. This cannot be possible when social and economic objectives differ from one country to another. It is only if accounting models based upon accounting objectives are compatible with one another that there is any real prospect of arriving at meaningful common standards. As McComb (1979) points out, "if any two national accounting models are irreconcilable, then either one or both must be fundamentally changed if common standards are assumed to be a primary goal".

Chetkovich (1972) states "it would make sense that we seek to define international accounting objectives before we attempt to define international accounting standards. Common objectives must necessarily derive from social and economic environments that are similar and thus create similar needs". Chetkovich agrees that research and the spread of ideas could mean that accountants in one country benefit from the experience of others, but this does not mean that the results of research and discussions in one country will necessarily apply to another. Accounting in a country needs to develop in a manner relevant to the society in which it exists.

Gambling (1971) when discussing a general theory of accounting makes a comment on the possibilities of harmonization. "Conventional accounting practice has been dictated by the requirements of western industrial capitalism". The accounting practices of industrialised countries have been concerned with recording what is happening to private wealth, that is transferable wealth; it has not been concerned with public wealth. This public wealth based on such factors as education, health and culture has been ignored.

On the same theme as above, Queenan (1965) points to the problem of different environments leading to different attitudes and objectives:" The European businessman believes very strongly that it is good business to set aside a part of profits in a good year for use in bolstering profits in a bad year. This is in fact, creating secret reserves". In many leading industrial countries, this practice is seen as normal and it would take very much more than appeals to the conceptual framework of accounting to get businessmen to change a practice which they consider good and useful. The political aspects of accounting standards setting mean that the views of groups more powerful than accountants have to be allowed for.

Indeed, in some countries the US and UK levels of disclosure might be seen to the profession as harmful. Whether for tax purposes or some other, the business community may wish to limit disclosure. W. Sycip (1981) doubts whether "the needs of domestic companies in each country can be served by the same international standards domestically as they could be internationally".

Briston (1978) in a particularly hard-hitting article criticises harmonization on the grounds that the way it is going is not meeting the needs of developing countries: "Instead of recognising the inadequacies of the UK and US system and attempting to make it more relevant and integrated, UK and US accountants are gradually imposing that outmoded system upon developing countries. On the contrary, developing countries must create their own systems before this adverse influence has reached an irreversible stage. Each country should be encouraged not to standardise the structure and specifications of its information system, but to create a system appropriate to its own needs". "At present, the worldwide tendency is in exactly the opposite direction". Briston traces the spread of Western accounting ideas throughout the world. British influence is very longstanding in many old-colonial countries. He points out that once a reporting system and nucleus of an accounting profession has been established, it becomes very difficult to modify the system. Those who run it have a vested interest. The result is that these countries have adopted accounting principles and systems which originally evolved to meet the needs of UK capitalism.

As well as tracing the British influence through Nigeria and other British areas of influence Briston also makes reference to the Dutch influence on the accounting profession in Indonesia. He argues for an alternative system and bases this argument on the ideas advanced by Enthoven. Enthoven (1970) defines three major areas of accounting, namely, Enterprise Accounting, (which includes Financial Accounting, Management Accounting and Auditing), Governmental Accounting and Social Accounting. He stresses the need to integrate all of these areas into a single accounting framework.

Briston's point is that the UK and US system does not attempt to do this. The attempts at harmonization based on the UK and US system are really only concerned with enterprise accounting.

An interesting country case study showing the difficulties of harmonizing, when societies are developing and changing, is that the USSR. In 1926 a Soviet delegation attended the International Accounting Congress held in Amsterdam. A few years later Soviet delegations visited an accounting machine exhibition in Paris and a number of German industrial concerns. At the time Russian accounting specialists argued that the principles of accounting were not affected by socio-economic factors. This view dominated the publications and teaching of accounting in Russia in the 1920's. It was argued that the principles of accounting applied whatever the economic system. The accountants holding this view were however being criticised by some for purveying bourgeois accounting theories.

In 1929 the Party Conference adopted a five year plan and took the decision to develop a unified system of national economic accounting. The inward flow of West Europe an accounting thought and practice ceased, the European connection was severed. The reason for this change was that the objectives, the accounting information needed, had been reassessed. A new journal entitled "For Socialist Accounting" was launched with articles appearing on such topics as a Trotskist views of the role of accounting in a socialist society (Bailey 1984).

Abel (1971) presents the case of Germany in the 1930's to illustrate that the environment is an important factor in determining the characteristics of any given set of national accounting practices. At that time Germany developed its own branch of uniform accounting in response to the economic and political conditions prevailing in the country. The success or failure of that system can be judged only in the context of the social and economic framework within which it operated. The point being that we should not judge the accounts produced to satisfy the domestic needs of a country by how they satisfy international investors or by the extent that they satisfy the standards of another country.

"Any attempt to compare those early German developments with other extensively similar efforts, such as the current American drive for greater uniformity in financial statement presentation, would seem quite improper as long as the different objectives of the respective accounting processes and differences in the environment are not given adequate consideration" (Abel 1971). The point being made is that one cannot expect harmonization if there are different social and economic frameworks.

In Germany in the 1930's the ready acceptance of state intervention in economic affairs and the tradition of anti-individualism, lead to a rapid increase in demand for capital funds which lead to strong banks, rather than businesses financed by promoters. Consequently, the practices of German banks began to differ markedly from those of their Anglo-Saxon counterparts. There tended to develop a system of information channelling separate from the usual published financial statements. The banks were interested in uniformity at the industrial level. This was needed by the State as well as the banks. Abel makes the point that the German experience has remained a strong factor in formulating continental European thinking on accounting. He believes that there are good and sound reasons why there should be some diversity in international accounting practices.

An interesting paper by Jaggi (1973) on the Impact of the Cultural Environment on Financial Disclosures deals with problems of harmonizing standards. He concludes "this study also indicates that cultural differences within the economically developed countries will dictate differences in the development of accounting principles in these countries. Therefore it is important that the development of international accounting standards recognises this and gives adequate consideration to the impacts of cultural environments on financial disclosures".

Jaggi makes reference to the paper by Mahon (1965) in which the point is made that statements prepared in developing countries are less reliable than those in economically developed countries. It is believed, however, by Jaggi that as capital markets in these countries develop as the supply of private capital grows, the need for reliable information will become more crucial. Shuaib (1978) and (1981) explains that no attempt has yet been made in Kuwait to develop accounting practices to suit the environment of that country.

Gaertner and Rueschhoff (1980) offer an interesting but unlikely possibility. They are concerned with the cultural barriers that stand in the way of international standards, and in particular, with language problems, different attitudes towards disclosure, and a general resistance to change. They go on to say that "historically, many leading scholars such as Socrates and Einstein have described themselves as ... members of a society that could easily be characterised as an international subculture. Through the efforts of IASC such an international subculture, superimposed on national cultures may evolve and help to solve the cultural dilemma for international investors".

Beazley (1968) raises the question, "do we need national accounting and auditing standards before we have national standards? Or are international standards a more reasonable premise with which to begin". He makes reference to the article by Bedford (1966) in which the distinction is made between the flow of technical information and the flow of accounting thought. Often an international discussion begins with accountants describing the practices in their own country, but this leads to a discussion on objectives and leads to what can be described as an international flow of accounting thoughts. Perhaps it is possible to reach agreement at an international level, but not at a national level.

Beazley makes the point that "until all members of the international profession have a common understanding of their role in society, the assumptions upon which economic activity rests, the nature of human economic motivation and the validity and usefulness of common measurement methods, there can be no well organised international accounting". Beazley is in favour of international discussions and the international flow of ideas. The basic premise of his 1968 paper is that research efforts should focus primarily on the cross-cultural aspects of the operation of accountants in different environments.

As Choi and Mueller (1978) state "If we then accept the proposition that the environments in which accounting operates are not the same in different countries or even in different organisations, it stands to reason that accounting must necessarily differ from case to case if it is to retain the sharp cutting edge of social utility".

Fantl (1971) makes a similar point. "World accountants today need to begin to act in concert, to join together in programs that not only examine and reconcile their differences, but also explain the means of broadening world understanding of accounting and its critical role in progress". Indeed "the growth of multi-national business interests and the expansion of governmental and quasi-governmental assistance makes the prospect of compatible worldwide accounting most appealing". "Unfortunately the solution is too simple and the problem too complex". Accounting diversity is a fact of life. While accounting methods may continue to improve (particularly in developing countries) uniformity is not likely to be a dominant factor in the evolutionary process.

The 1970's were good years for standards, both at a national level and international level. Many standards were produced and the rank and file in the profession seemed to accept that this was necessary. The 1980's appear to be different. Standards have to be paid for and increasingly questions are being asked as to whether some of the standards are particularly useful and whether all the effort and expense is worthwhile. In the UK in 1982 the ICAEW only agreed on the strength of a very small majority to continue to apply SSAP 16 for the remaining years of its trial period. Falk (1980) asks the question in Canada "do we really need accounting and auditing standards. We seem to be paying more and benefitting less". The same question could be asked about international standards.

One obstacle to harmonization raised by many authors is nationalism. Arpan and Radebaugh (1981) believe that "nationalism, egoism and pride also impede progress: the French would like to have the new global system patterned after the French system... the Americans the American. Each country believes its system is the best and is reluctant to adopt a system it perceives to be inferior or unsuitable". Fantl (1971) also argued that some countries would be unwilling to accept compromises if it involved changing their existing accounting practices.

The final argument against harmonization that will be considered, is the one that developing countries have different needs for their accounting system to those of developed countries. It is of course true that accounting is necessary for economic development under any economic system. Why should the needs of developing countries be different?

Enthoven has done much to draw attention to the lack of attention to accounting problems in developing countries. He draws attention to the fact that "Accounting - mainly associated with enterprise accounting - is rarely fully appreciated as a profession, and accountants are often equated with bookkeepers. One of the most conspicuous and least justified impediments to the proper development of accounting is that it is not accepted as a valid instrument for measuring, processing and communicating information and formulating decisions in the micro and macro economic sectors. Few governments express public concern for, ... the establishment of sound accounting standards. The absence of such standards and the lack of uniform practices limit not only the safeguards and controls over credit and investments, and the related ability to call up financial resources when necessary, but also curtail the usefulness of accounting for managerial and decision making purposes in all sectors". (Enthoven 1981). Similar points have been made by amongst others: Levievre and Levievre (1978), and Solomons (1980).

The role of accounting in the development process is returned to in a later chapter. The concern at this point is whether the international harmonization of accounting will help or hinder economic development. Baccouchi (1969) points out that developing countries urgently need help, they usually do not have a generally accepted body of accounting principles and practices. He quotes the Tunisian experience to illustrate his point. When referring to international accounting, he clearly means the spread of ideas, the possible harmonization. He points out that developing countries "cannot afford to duplicate research, and most importantly, repeat errors". Linowes (1969) makes a similar case.

It would clearly save developing countries much time and cost if they adopted ready made standards. An examination of the origins of the existing accounting systems in most developing countries reveals that the systems were for the most part introduced by foreigners or foreign trained nationals, either as the result of colonial administration, foreign study or foreign investment. Wilkinson (1965) draws attention to the fact that in the past "the accounting principles of one country have never been 'sold' to another country on the basis of convincing arguments in support of those principles".

Briston (1978) has similarly noted that in Indonesia, as a result of the influence of multinational companies, international firms of accountants, and United States aid, university accounting courses became strongly biased toward American texts and that the Indonesian Institute of

Accountants adopted a set of accounting and auditing standards which were virtually identical to those of the USA. No doubt more examples could be cited but the point being made is that most developing countries had little chance to evolve accounting systems which truly reflected the needs and circumstances of their own societies. Their existing systems are largely extensions of those in developed countries. In this light, the benefits of their being more deeply integrated into systems that predominantly suit developed countries become questionable. For the Third World, international harmonization may do more harm than good if it pre-empts the possibility of changing the old, inappropriate systems and evolving new ones, better-suited to their development needs.

Enthoven pointed out in 1973, if accounting "Is to play useful and effective role in society, (it) must not pursue independent goals. It must continue to serve the objectives of its economic environment". He points out that we must not assume that what might be good accounting for the developed countries "will automatically be economically relevant and good for the emerging nations and the process of development".

At the same time as there are increasing calls to harmonize accounting principles and practices, there is an increasing interest, reflected in the literature, on the needs in developing countries, for information, some of it accounting information. The move towards harmonization does not necessarily mean that the information needs of developing countries will be satisfied. It is true the United Nations are trying to increase the level of disclosure of transnational companies and this would benefit the LDCs. There is, however, more to the question of the need for accounting information in LDCs, than just the disclosure of multinational companies. Seidler (1968) advanced the thesis that "the strength and extent of a nations information system determines in large part the rate at which economic development will progress and that accounting systems thus assume an important role in the development of emerging nations".

It can be argued that the application of lessons learned in one country to the problems of another country can lead to confusion. Economic development is a complex process. As Seidler (1968) points out, to conceive economic development by taking only a few variables, as has been the case in some developing countries and ignoring the other factors would not help to solve the economic evils of underdeveloped countries.

Samuels and Oliga (1982) question the rationale and desirability of broadening international accounting standards to encompass the Third World. They argue that differences between countries can be so great that the problem of appropriate accounting standards can assume vastly different conceptual meanings and contextual significance from one country to another. Bailey (1982) makes a similar point. In the 1960's there was a presumption that it was possible to transfer technology, including accounting procedures, from the major industrialised countries to other countries. Now more attention is being paid to the fitness of the technology for the purposes. We have become more aware of its inapposite qualities. Bailey (1982) argues "there may not be an accounting model universally applicable in all countries".

f) Supranational Agencies and International Bodies

A number of international bodies and committees are now concerned with harmonization and increasing levels of disclosure. Some of these are involved with the issue on a global scale, others at a regional level. Some of them involve discussions between representatives of national governments and others involve discussions between representatives of national accounting associations. For a survey of all such bodies see Brennan (1981). This section will consider the work of these bodies and committees. For convenience they will be divided between those primarily interested in global rather than regional issues and those that are public bodies rather than private.

(i) Global Bodies - Public

The UN and the OECD have become increasingly interested in the activities of transnational businesses. Both bodies are inter-governmental. Discussions that take place in these forums involve representatives of national governments. Because of their interests in multinational businesses, world trade and international investment, they are interested in accounting practices, in particular levels of disclosure. The progress that has been made by these bodies towards a code for multinational companies and towards international harmonization has already been discussed in section (b) of this chapter. For a review of their work see Benson 1973, Sahlgren 1979, Heath 1979, and Fitzgerald and Kelley 1979.

(ii) Global Bodies - Private

The IASC and the IFAC were considered earlier in the chapter. They each consist of representatives of professional accounting bodies from a large number of countries. They are private bodies. The 12th International Congress held in Mexico in 1982 saw agreement reached on a form of cooperation between these two bodies, with agreement on mutual commitment. The private bodies would like to establish a working relationship with the intergovernmental agencies, but at the moment there would appear to still be a long way to go.

(iii) Regional Bodies - Public

The last 30 years has seen the formation of a number of regional economic communities. Many countries have agreed to work more closely together hoping it will strengthen theeconomies and the industry of the countries concerned. One of the principle objectives of these communities is to promote the development of economic activity between member states. This involves harmonising laws, and eventually bringing together as much as possible of accounting practices. The progress that has been made on the accounting side will now be considered.

European Economic Community

The EEC has made some progress toward its goal of harmonization. (See Burnett, 1975, Nobes, 1980 and Gray and Coenenberg 1984) The Fourth Directive has meant that most member countries now have a common format in their annual accounts. Gray and Coenenberg (1984) contains a series of papers dealing with the implementation of the Fourth Directive in member countries. The UK and Denmark at the time led in the implementation process, with Italy lagging behind all other countries. A number of problems of harmonization with the community are considered, including the difficulty with the 'true and fair view' concept which of course leads to problems in countries with a strong legislative tradition. A proposed Seventh Directive on consolidated accounts has run into problems and some of its initial suggestions have had to be abandoned.

The extent to which the adoption of the Directives by member countries will lead to harmonization is a debatable issue. Nobes (1980) when discussing the Fourth Directive argues that "substantial diversity (both between and within countries) will still be possible within the national laws which will eventually be passed. Supporters of the view that rigid uniformity merely masks a multitude of differences will be happy with this".

Regional inter-governmental bodies clearly have the power to enforce harmonization, should they wish to do so. One can see why the international bodies representing the accounting profession are keen to work closely with inter-governmental bodies. In Europe it is the Groupe d'Etudes des Experts Comptables that assists the EEC in its deliberations. (See Rutteman 1983). In fact as Daley and Mueller (1982) point out "only one international organisation presently promulgating accounting standards has the ability to enforce its recommendations"; that organisation being the EEC. The work of the UN is still ongoing, and at present we do not know what the results will be .

Coleman (1981) discusses the development of accounting standards in the EEC and makes the point that in his view accounting and reporting rules for business are now sensitive political issues, they are no longer essentially of private concern: "The question now is not whether a rule is good, bad or indifferent, but who exercised the power to make the rule and in whose interest was it made".

Africa

Another region of the world that has an international association of accountants, made up of government representatives, is Africa. One of the lesser known inter-governmental organisations, the African Accounting Council (AAC), was founded in 1979. Its objectives include the harmonization of accounting systems in African countries and the promotion and carrying out of research into accounting standardisation. One of the problems they will encounter in their efforts to harmonise is that because of the colonial past, they have two main accounting models in existence on the continent, namely the British and the French (Enthoven 1981).

Its first Congress was held in Algiers in 1979, its second in Lagos in 1982, at which the theme was "Accounting in Africa, Past, Present and Future". It has aims relating to training and a number of forms of cooperation. A permanent secretariat has been established in Zaire. Although the 1982 Congress did not make much progress on the harmonization issue, they were able to initiate a number of measures relating to the training of accountants. In future greater attention will be paid in individual countries to the "African dimension" of accounting needs.

(iv) Regional Bodies - Private

There are four well established private regional bodies that hold regular meetings and each of these will now be briefly considered. In addition to these four there are other regional bodies that occasionally meet.

(a) Inter-American Accounting Conference (A.I.C.)

The first Inter-American Accounting Conference was held in Puerto Rico in 1949. Since then a number of conferences have been held. The fifth Conference had been scheduled for Havana, Cuba (1959), but due to political developments was cancelled.

The fundamental objectives of the Inter-American Accounting Conferences have been discussed by Elliott (1968). A number of sub-committees have existed during the life of A.I.C., one of which was concerned with terminology. The objectives of the sub-committee included unifying accounting terms in America, and compiling a dictionary of accounting terms in English, Spanish and Portuguese. Another sub-committee has been concerned with the interchange of students and professors among member countries. Yet another sub-committee deals with accounting principles and standards.

Elliot writing in 1968 on the work of the Conference up to that time concludes that "A review of the efforts expended by the various sub-committees of the Inter-American Accounting Conference indicates that a great desire to obtain accounting uniformity in the countries of the Western Hemisphere exists. The economic logic and necessity for such uniformity cannot be over-estimated. Trade and investments are no longer confined to the borders of a given national entity; today they are practiced at an international level. As a result, the uniformity of accounting practices and the consequent comparability of the financial statement are highly desirable".

"To obtain this uniformity, the USA must exercise a dominant role, since, in the Western Hemisphere, it is the country in which accounting development has been greatest". "The uniformity which is sought is vital for the economic progress of Latin America. Confidence must be instilled in private investors so that Latin America will attract its share of private capital". "The work of the Inter-American Accounting Conference is highly desirable because it is one of the most direct means of influencing the proper development of accounting in the Latin American area".

Reference is again made in this quotation to the logic and necessity for uniform accounting. The argument to support this being that trade and investment are "no longer" confined to the borders of a given national entity; today they are practised at an international level. Elliott's conclusions undoubtedly have much support. They do, however, appear to be somewhat heavy handed. As discussed elsewhere in this chapter developing countries may have special accounting needs. The US accounting system is arguably the best in the world, but its main objective does seem to be to satisfy the needs of shareholders. Developing countries have other perhaps equally important needs.

Latin America has attracted a large amount of private capital. It has resulted in many problems. There is much more to international investment than accounting standards. One barrier to international harmonization that is often mentioned is "nationalism". Nationalism can work in two ways, what is usually meant by the expression in the international accounting literature, is the reluctance of a country to abandon its own methods in favour of a new internationally agreed standard approach. Nationalism can also mean, the belief that ones own methods are so superior that everyone else should adopt them.

An interesting example of the spread of accounting ideas between countries arose as a result of the meeting of the Inter-American Accounting Conference held in October 1970 in Bogota. This was the ninth conference and it dealt specifically with issues of inflation adjusted accounting. It was resolved that the member organisations should take the necessary steps in their respective countries to ensure that general price level adjusted financial statements be published as complementary information to traditional financial statements. Argentina was the first country to adopt the recommendations followed by Chile. Argentina's pronouncements on inflation adjusted accounts were approved in November 1972 but their implementation delayed. Chile in December 1974 introduced changes in tax and accounting practices.

(b) U.E.C. Union Européene des Experts Comptables, Economiques et Financiers

This body was founded in 1951. There had been discussion at the time about creating an 'International Institute of Accounting' under the aegis of UNESCO, but such a body did not materialise. Instead, a European body was created, which has a membership of professional bodies from over 20 countries. Despite its 30 year history and its wide membership it has however not had much of an impact: "Very few accountants outside the upper echelons of the big audit firms have any clear idea of what UEC actually does" (World Accounting Report, December 1982). It was described as a baby brother of IFAC, but is is, of course, much older than IFAC, a body formed in 1977 at the 11th International Congress of Accountants held in Munich. Coincidentally the secretariat of the UEC is in Munich.

The first Congress of UEC was held in Florence and Rome in 1953. It had as its theme 'Accounting Uniformity and Economic Integration'. The Congress set up a permanent commission to investigate the feasibility of a European Chart of Accounts, for at the time charts of accounts were seen as the vehicle for harmonising accounting practices. At the 5th Congress held in Vienna in 1964, two technical papers on the subject of a European Uniform Chart of Accounts were discussed. The progress made is reported by Kafer (1965).

In 1963 the membership of UEC was considerably enlarged. This initially changed the orientation of the UEC in that activities aimed at harmonization within the profession had to be slowed down whilst further comparative studies were undertaken. In 1966 the Journal of the UEC was launched.
At the 6th Congress held in Copenhagen in 1969 a paper on the progress made during the 18 years of

the UEC was presented, and this was subsequently published in the Journal (October 1969).

In April 1972 the UEC was reorganised, it had not up to then produced the desired results with regard to harmonization. Perhaps it was not possible to do so as the Congress was an organisation made up of national professional accounting bodies, and the Congress could not act independently of these member bodies. In the 1970's the UEC began work on recommendations on accounting and auditing issues. In 1974 the first set of recommendations were produced on the subject of accounting disclosure and auditing requirements (UEC Journal, April 1974). A number of other recommendations and exposure drafts followed, mostly on auditing topics (Perridon 1975).

In 1978 the first four definitive UEC statements were published. By 1981 the Auditing Statements Board had produced 14 Exposure Drafts. The UEC is not, however, just a standard setting body, it has had many sub-committees concerned with a wide range of topics (UEC Journal, January 1975). The October 1976 edition of the Journal, had an article on the 25 years of the UEC. It pointed out the UEC was empowered by its constitution "to take every initiative appropriate to create a spirit of solidairty amongst the accountants of European countries".

Another aspect of accounting cooperation in Europe is the bilateral discussion that takes place. In 1972 the first Anglo-German Seminar of accountants took place. In 1973 a German-French Seminar was held, this was followed by numerous other bilateral meetings including Dutch-German, Franco-British and Anglo-Scandinavian. All of these seminars covered topics of mutual interest.

At the 11th Congress of the UEC, Reydel, the President, presented a paper on the "Harmonization of Accounting and Auditing Practice in the last 5 years'. He said "We salute the creation of the IFAC, but we are convinced that it will only be able to achieve its objective if it arranges to lean, as envisaged in its constitution, on the experience of the regional organisations, and if it respects the individualities of its members". Clearly, the position was changing with new international bodies being formed. The UEC has had a life of over 30 years, but its impact appears to have been minimal. In October 1980 the Journal of the UEC had to close down through lack of support. It was pointed out when announcing the closure that much had changed over the last five years with the IASC, and the IFAC having affected the basic role of the journal.

The UEC is a different body to the Group d'Etudes des Experts Comptables de la CEE, which is a study group made up of representatives of all the professional bodies of the member states of the EEC. The primary task of this later body is to represent the profession in the development and harmonization discussions within the EEC. It also advises the EEC on issues discussed at the UN and OECD relating to international accounting (Rutteman 1983).

(c) Association of South East Asian Nations Federation of Accountants (AFA)

This is a regional accounting body, covering five South East Asian countries, namely Indonesia, Malaysia, Phillippines, Thailand and Singapore. It was formed in March 1977, held its first conference in 1978, the second in 1980, and third in 1982.

Choi (1980) has referred to it as a new international accounting force. Speaking at the second conference S.T.C. Chuan, the then President of the Singapore Society of Accountants, stated "For the longer term objective it may even be possible to gradually harmonise accounting and auditing standards and practices in the ASEAN region. The task is not an easy one. Owing to the differences in history, culture and political systems the accounting and auditing practices in the ASEAN countries vary from country to country". He made reference to the contribution accountants can make in stimulating economic development and in particular in assisting their clients with the development of investment projects.

L.K.C. Wong who at the time was President of AFA, referred to the fact that AFA had in 1979 produced its first accounting standard, which was on the subject of fundamental accounting principles, and in 1980 produced its first auditing standard. He explained, however, that although AFA had issued these standards that member countries should not be seen as going their own way, issuing purely ASEAN standards: "We have IFAC auditing standards, we have IASC accounting standards. We have our own. Who do we follow?" He explained that accountants in member countries would continue to peg their accounting and auditing standards to both IASC and IFAC promulgations. But as these are seen as minimum standards for consumption for the whole world, AFA would modify these standards to suit their own practical requirements. Some of the standards or parts of the standards of IASC and IFAC did not apply to the member countries of AFA. On the other hand member countries had particular problems of their own, for example, valuing tin, rubber and other commodities (ASEAN Federation 1981). In addition to standards, AFA is also interested in working towards common educational standards, and in developing a code of ethics applicable to member countries.

(d) Confederation of Asian and Pacific Accountants (CAPA)

This is another private accounting body in South East Asia. The President of CAPA speaking at the 2nd Conference of the other South East Asian body (AFA) said that CAPA was currently having discussions on its role. "What should be the role of CAPA in the standard setting policies around the world? Should we do something like IFAC, like IASC, like what (sic) some national bodies and some regional bodies are doing? We think it may not be practical to do so... we may only duplicate efforts that are being properly handled by world bodies" (Villanueva, in ASEAN Proceedings, 1981).

CAPA is an older body than AFA. It held its first conference in Manila in 1957. Speaking at the Fourth Conference of CAPA held in New Delhi in 1965, Deering spoke of the need to enhance "the degree to which financial statements prepared in any area of the world can be made acceptable and understood in every other area of the world". He pointed out that it was necessary to work for a better understanding of the accounting principles and standards of each country and referred to the Fourth CAPA Conference and others like it as "sounding boards" for better communication and understanding. At the Eighth CAPA Conference held in Hong Kong in 1976 an interesting session was held on "The Emergence of International Accounting Standards in the face of diverging national accounting standards".

(e) Middle East Society of Associated Accountants

Enthoven (1981) makes reference to this regional society. Unfortunately it has been dormant for some time and, as it was organised out of Beirut, it is unlikely to be active again in the near future. It held the first Accounting Congress of the Middle East in 1965, and in 1970, was producing generally accepted auditing standards.

(f) Commonwealth Conference of Accountants

The first such conference was held in India in 1975. Although it does not seem to have resulted in an active body being formed, this first conference did attract 1,400 delegates.

(g) Conclusions on Work of International Bodies

The public bodies whether global or regional could have an important impact on accounting. The EEC is already introducing changes in methods of financial reporting. Such bodies have the political power to effect changes and to ensure that their wishes are carried out. The private bodies are important in that they are meeting places where views can be expressed and ideas exchanged. It is possible that the private bodies will work closely with the public bodies, this is certainly the direction in which most of them appear to wish to move.

Most research papers on the committees and congresses must by the nature of the subject be descriptive. There are a few interesting papers on decision making processes within these bodies. There is a paper by Daley and Mueller (1982) in which country representation on international standard setting bodies is analysed. Of the countries who are represented on at least three of the bodies, 7 are Western developed nations, only one is from Africa, and none are from the Middle East. They point out that because of the "Western bias" of the IASC many of the developing nations criticise its work for "being insensitive to their situation and needs". Daley and Mueller conclude that if private sector standard setting is to continue as at present, with no enforcement powers, then it must become more internationally oriented. By this they mean that more nations must be represented on the international committees than at present; it is then more likely that statements will be acceptable.

One conclusion of the Nair and Frank (1981) study is that accounting practices in the USA seem to serve as a model for the increasing level of international harmonization that they observed. Undoubtedly the USA leads in standard setting, and this is why Nair and Frank found that "the practices which the rest of the world had moved towards requiring (or prohibiting) by 1979 had already been required (or prohibited) in the USA in 1975".

Following the USA will lead to a certain degree of harmonization, but not to the goal of universal accounting standards that some writers would like to see. Pomeranz (1981) rightly questions whether the "disclosure requirements in the US - based on the perceived information needs of investors and creditors - answer the very special needs of users abroad (outside the USA) such as governments and trade unions".

Mueller (1979) bravely attempts to assess the impact of the International Congresses of Accountants. One conclusion he comes to is that they "have become prime carriers of the Anglo-American conventional accounting model". He makes the point that the IASC also seems to be moving along the same path. "There seems little doubt the Anglo-American type of financial accounting is much more widespread in 1979 than it was only a decade or two ago".

As was demonstrated in Chapter Two of the book accounting has a long and illustrious international heritage. Mueller mentions that it turned nationalistic towards the end of the nineteenth century, when professional standards and practices became divided along political boundaries. Mueller (1979) believes that International Congresses have helped to restore the balance between the different interest groups. They have certainly helped in the understanding of the alternative systems. It is to be hoped that the increasing awareness of the international aspects of the subjects results in truly international attempts to advance the subject.

Chapter Five

INTERNATIONAL DIMENSIONS OF ACCOUNTING AND FINANCIAL REPORTING PRACTICE

a) Introduction

The title of this chapter is taken from Mueller's 1967 book on International Accounting. Books on multinational accounting and finance tend to divide this subject into four areas, these being:

(a) Accounting Reporting Problems

(b) Management Information Systems and Control

(c) Financial Management and Planning, and

(d) International Tax Problems

The latter two areas lie outside the scope of this book. The literature on the first two topics is vast. Agami and Kollaritsch (1983) in a bibliography on international accounting covering the literature published in the period from 1972 to 1981, devote 60 pages to articles on financial reporting problems and 50 pages to articles on management accounting issues. The survey below can only be illustrative of what has been written on these two topics.

b) Accounting Reporting Problems

There are many accounting problems with an international aspect that could be considered, but this section will limit itself to just three of these, namely currency translation, multiple reports and segmental reports. Others which could have been considered in a larger text include for example, acccounting for global inflation.

The accounting problems discussed under this heading are those that result from the international aspects of business. Two sets of problems can be identified, those that arise in reporting international operations in home country financial statements, and those that arise in reporting the business activities within the host country. The first set of problems are very much a domestic matter of the home country and in most developed countries have been the subject of numerous articles and some research. The second set of problems have until recently received less attention, but are now of much concern to such supra-national agencies as the UN and OECD.

The involvement in international activities arise because the business is transnational and invests outside its home country, or merely because it trades with foreign countries. There are clearly many practical accounting problems that arise when a business is international. Such problems as the consolidation of overseas subsidiaries and the translation of foreign currency financial statements are major issues. Although the problems are concerned with international operations, the solutions adopted are usually those that conform to the national practices or standards of the home country of the enterprise.

The financial reporting issues and problems are well covered in the literature dealing with domestic accounting problems and in the literature on accounting for multinational business (see for example Moore and Scott (1973), Rueschhoff (1976), Al Hashim and Robertson (1978) and Arpan and Radebaugh (1981).

There is a vast literature in most countries on just the one issue of consolidation of foreign subsidiaries. Also most books dealing with accounting for multinational companies, multinational business and international accounting have one or more sections on consolidated accounts. For example, Watt, Hammer and Burge (1977) all partners in Price Waterhouse, in their book on Multinational Corporations, discuss consolidation practices. They in fact do not like the Continental European approach which can result in consolidating subsidiaries where there is less than 51% ownership. They believe that in order to ensure that control over the resources of the investee is not just temporary, it is necessary to have the 51% share ownership, and that one should not consolidate unless one is sure control is permanent, and this is best measured by ownership of a majority of the ordinary, or equity share capital.

Further comparative work is to be found in the Price Waterhouse surveys (1973, 1976, 1980) where details of consolidation practices in many countries are given and to which reference has already been made in earlier chapters. The Accountants International Study Group (1973) discussed consolidation practice in the three participating countries. The UEC Auditing Committee (1978) produced a study on the preparation and audit of consolidated statements. Ernst and Whinney (1980) was an excellent study comparing consolidated accounting practices in different European countries and a good example of the publications from the public accounting firms. Nobes and Parker (1981) discuss the differences in the laws relating to consolidation in the USA, the UK, France, Germany and the Netherlands. They draw attention to the important legal differences, as well as differences of practice. These different conceptual approaches can be identified as parent company, entity and proprietry.

There are also many practical differences, some reflecting the different view taken of overseas subsidiaries. This has caused the EEC problems in their efforts to produce a directive on group accounts (the Seventh Directive) and the Arthur Young McClelland Moores(1983) publication provides an up to date summary of the existing law and practice in the EEC countries and the changes they will have to introduce (McKinnon 1983).

The rest of this chapter will concentrate more on the literature which emphasises the multinational business problems than on the literature on home country reporting.

i) Currency Translation

This is not a new problem, it has existed ever since one country traded with another. Earlier literature did not use the term 'translation' but used the term 'conversion' to describe both the actual exchange of one currency for another and the re-expression of financial data denominated in one currency in terms of another currency. The first process is a real transaction but the second one is merely a pre-requisite for the preparation of consolidated statements for the group or easier reading. Baxter and Yamey (1951) remind us that "Like most other forms of advanced accounting, foreign branch accounts are much older than one might casually suppose. Thus the Fuggers had eleven foreign branches strung out all the way from Lisbon to

Dansig and the bookkeeper at their Augsberg Head Office has left us with a record (from 1518) of how he consolidated the branch returns into annual accounts for the whole undertaking". It is still a problem, as can be seen by the time it has taken the accounting standard bodies in the USA and UK to agree as to the most appropriate technique for translating financial statements prepared in one currency into another. Parker (1970) discusses why it would have been difficult to obtain agreement between countries as to the most appropriate method given the methods available at that time.

During the 1950s and 1960s when most exchange rates applied in international trade were fixed there was not much discussion. Following the devaluation of sterling against the United States dollar in November 1967 there was the need for guidance. Recommendation N25 of the ICAEW "The Accounting treatment of major changes in the sterling parity of overseas currencies", required the identification of the exceptional gain or loss, its segregation from normal gains or losses and its disclosure as a separate exceptional item. This could be in computing the profit or loss of the period, below the 'profit after taxation' or "in so far as the loss or gain is regarded as not being of a revenue nature it may be dealt with by direct transfer to or from reserve". The two main methods used for translation at this time were the 'closing rate' and 'historic rate' which required long term liabilities to be translated at the rate ruling when they were incurred. The last paragraph of the Appendix is interesting as it compares the development and acceptability of these two rates: "The 'historic rate' was evolved in the context of overseas branches and subsidiaries largely financed and stocked from the United Kingdom". The 'closing rate' recognises "overseas branches and subsidiaries as viable units existing apart from their parent". Perhaps this is the birth of the 'net investment concept' which although considered in subsequent research and discussion did not have any significant impact on an accounting standard until much later.

Nobes (1980) reviews the translation debate and the development from the closing rate through current/non-current, monetary/non-monetary to the temporal principle which was adopted as the basis of FAS No 8 (1975). Dissatisfaction arose as it became apparent that economic (real) risk and subsequent profit or loss were not being adequately reflected by the accounting measurement method, or more particularly the requirement to include all losses or gains in the income statement. In the United Kingdom the ASC had not been able to agree on a standard so a major step towards international harmonization took place when representatives of the standard setting authorities met to consider the development of a mutually acceptable standard. These discussions eventually led to FAS No 52 (1981) and SSAP 20 (1983) and influenced CRS No 1650 (1983) and IAS 21 (1983). The first three require the identification of the organisational relationship between the home (parent) and overseas (subsidiary). If the overseas activity is an extension of the home activities (integrated) then the historic cost principles should be applied, i.e. use of the temporal method. If the overseas activity has an existence of its own, virtually independent of the parent company (self-sustaining), then it would be appropriate to treat it as a separate investment and translate the net amount of this investment at the closing rate. This does not mean that there is a choice of method. The method to be used follows directly from the relationship. The IAS 21 is not so specific and a choice can be made between the two methods.

There have been a number of studies on the impact of one translation method compared with that of another. One impressive piece of research on this topic is that of Burns (1976) who evaluated the economic consequences of SFAS No 8 and concluded that as a result of the standard multinational business had to increase their hedging and forward exchange transactions in the foreign currency markets and this added to their costs and so reduced their international competitiveness.

Evans and Folks (1979) also examined the response to SFAS No 8 and found it had a considerable impact on multinational companies. The economic impact of the standard was further examined by Shank, Dillard and Murdock (1979). The standards impact on managerial risk management was examined by Evans, Folks and Jilling (1978). As a result of this type of research, and the resulting criticisms of the standard No 8, the FASB introduced a new standard.

Further research on this topic is that by Dukes (1978) who investigated the effects on security price behaviour of the different currency translation methods, and by Aggarwal (1980) who investigated the effects of currency translation and conversion on the reported profitability of multinational companies.

There are numerous economic theories on rates of exchange, for example the Fisher theory and the purchasing power parity theory. The accounting methods of foreign currency translation can be tested against these theories. This is one area of international accounting where rigorous research is being undertaken. Accounting and Business Research devoted 25 pages to this topic with Patz (1977) "A price parity theory of translation", a comment by Flower (1978), a reply by Patz (1978) and a further article by Clarke (1978) whose conclusion was: "Parities are not alternatives to exchange rates. At best, they are surrogates for them. Exchange rates are prices. Whether they equate with parities is of no consequence in so far as translation is the matter of concern".

The above references are indicative of recent work on currency translation. There are many older articles. In the third edition of Kubin and Mueller's Bibliography (1973) there are over 160 references to articles on foreign currency translation. It must be emphasised however, that most of these articles are concerned with the problems for domestic reporting practices of currency translation resulting from international business operations.

As a practical accounting problem the quoted multinational companies have followed the rules promulgated by the authorities they wish to satisfy. Almost by definition a multinational company will want its shares to be quoted on the New York Stock Exchange as well as on a European one. They became a strong pressure group on the standard setting bodies of the US, UK and Europe to agree on a common standard. The Royal Dutch Shell group in its 1977 report (issued April 1978) said "There is cause for concern, however, at the present fast increasing flow of proposed new requirements, some of doubtful value to the user, which threatens the financial reporting of international companies with a complexity which can obscure the important issues" and "Support will also be given to the efforts of the IASC to harmonize the different standards that at present exist worldwide and to achieve acceptance from national and international authorities for its standards".

In its 1978 Report the Company said "The absence of international agreement on an appropriate method for accounting in a period of high inflation is a matter for continuing concern" and in the 1980 Report "The publication in 1980 of broadly similar draft accounting standards in the UK and US on foreign currency translation was the result of close cooperation between accounting bodies on both sides of the Atlantic. This work has served as a valuable example for future efforts at harmonization in which other countries might take part".

Its report for 1983 was able to state "The accounting policies followed are consistent in all material respects with generally accepted accounting principles in each of the Netherlands, the United Kingdom and the United States, except for that in use in the United Kingdom in respect of deferred taxation".

The logic and potential simplicity of 'current values translated at current rates' has not found favour due to the practical problems of determining current values and the weight of tradition favouring the historical cost basis for the original financial data.

ii) Multiple Reports

Mueller and Walker (1976) in "The Coming of Age of Transnational Financial Reporting" argue that multinational business is the primary generator of transnational financial reporting needs. They see multinational businesses as continuing to grow in importance, therefore they see the need and requirements for transnational financial reporting as of increasing importance. They draw attention to a remark of Kapnick that this issue of world standards of accounting will not go away. Not only is there the host country requirements for increased disclosure, there are also the needs of shareholders in different countries. When the shares of a company are all held within one country then financial information requirements depend upon the principles of that country. Both those who prepare the accounts and those who use them know the rules. This is not the case with the international ownership of companies. The foreign shareholder may not know the local rules.

There are various ways in which this problem can be tackled. The Accountants International Study Group (1975) recommended that two kinds of financial statements be recognised as necessary: primary statements for a company's domestic users, and secondary statements for users of a company's accounts in other countries. The study group recognised that there would be a number of problems, for example, the secondary statements may be stated in different currency to the primary statement and there could be auditing difficulties with the secondary statements.

Choi (1980) has gone as far as to demonstrate that such statements have a potential to mislead users outside the domestic country. He suggests that secondary financial statements should be accompanied by environmental disclosures. Such disclosures would indicate which business and financial practices are common to the home country and the country of the users of the secondary statement and which practices are different.

An alternative approach to the problem would be single domicile reporting. In this the multinational company would merely convert and translate the consolidated financial statement from the currency and language of one country to the currency and language of another. These restatements and possible translations would be provided as a courtesy to users in foreign countries in an effort to try and improve communications. They would not however try to use the accounting principles of the user country. It has been argued that a financial statement can reflect only a single point of view and that has to be the country of the domicile company. It is being argued that it is too difficult or even impossible to reproduce the accounts and rework them according to the rules and conventions of each user country. This translation and conversion approach means the users of accounts in foreign countries would themselves have to obtain at least a general understanding of the accounting principles in the domicile countries.

Several multinational groups whose primary statements are expressed in French francs and follow French accounting standards issued versions of their financial statements in the English language and retained amounts in French francs. One example was BSN-GERVAIS DANONE which in its English Edition of the Annual report for 1978 stated "The consolidated financial statements have been prepared within the framework of principles defined in the report issued by the Conseil National de la Comptabilité with, however, some variations as indicated in the following notes".

The care needed when interpreting the accounts of a multinational is also emphasised by the discussion in the English language version of the Royal Dutch/Shell group of companies for 1983. "Currency factors again had a major impact on the reported earnings for all segments. While continued strengthening of the US dollar ... the net result was positive....... Additionally, the weakening of sterling against.... US dollar augmented Group earnings when aggregated in sterling... Shell Oil's (a US company) 1983 income.... was only 2% up... whereas its contribution to Group sterling earnings was 18% higher".

Numerous businessmen have written on the subject of the problems of multinational operations. Bowles (1968), who was at the time Comptroller of Dow Chemical, discusses the problems of reporting the operations of a large international group. He explains that where possible Dow and most U.S. companies follow practices within their foreign subsidiaries consistent with those practices in the U.S. Hunziker (1968), General Accountant at Caterpillar Tractor, commenting on the Bowles paper, stated "One of our continuing problems in the recording of foreign financial affairs is to strive for consistency so that our consolidated financial results are meaningful and permit comparisons between individual Caterpillar companies and profit centres". Other aspects of multiple reporting have been discussed in the Chapter on harmonization.

iii) Segmented Reporting

Increasingly, companies are being asked to disclosure certain information relating to their geographical activities. There is now a standard on this topic from the IASC. As well as domestic standards on this subject existing in a few countries there are also UN, OECD and EEC proposals and guidelines. These supranational bodies are considering the interest of the host countries and clearly disclosure of multinational operations is recognised as important from the host country's point of view.

There will probably continue to be considerable interest in this topic as the traditional 'home' countries are becoming 'host' countries. In both the United States and United Kingdom, Japanese companies, as well as each others, are responding to the incentives to investment or the perceived opportunities.

An early statement on dislcosing details of foreign operations appeared in a 1953 Bulletin of the AICPA. The point was made that "most foreign assets stand in some degree of jeopardy so far as ultimate realisation by US owners is concerned" therefore disclosure of foreign items is important.

Such disclosures are considered to be in the interests of the users in the home country. We therefore have had host and home country pressure for some disclosure of geographical activities.

In the 1960's in the USA there were numerous studies and statements on this topic. The difficulties of segmenting operations on a geographic basis were discussed by Mautz (1968). Backer and McFarland (1968) report that financial analysts can better assess risk when sales data is broken down on a country by country basis, or area by area basis. An AICPA research study by Lorensen (1972) pointed out that as US business was becoming increasingly international greater attention needed to be paid to geographical segmentation. The FASB issued a discussion document on this subject in 1974, an exposure draft in 1975, and a standard in 1976. The standard required certain information to be disclosed with regard to foreign operations and export sales.

The statement was not clear as to the form in which the information should be disclosed, for example, it did not say how narrow or how wide should be the geographical area. It left considerable freedom to management on this issue. Some countries just divided their foreign operations into two groups, for example, those in the Western Hemisphere and those in the Eastern Hemisphere; others divided their figures into groups on the basis of their activities in the different continents. The guidelines given for determining geographical segments were that the company should take into account "proximity, economic affinity, similarities in business environments, and nature, scale and degree of interrelationship of the enterprises' operations in the various countries". The information to be disclosed for each segment, was the revenue, the operating profit or loss, and the identifiable assets in that segment. The sales figure was to be broken down into sales within the group of companies and sales to unaffiliated customers. Companies were expected to reveal their policy on the sensitive issue of transfer pricing.

In the UK the Companies Act of 1967 required companies to disclose limited information for substantially different classes of business. They were required to show sales revenue and profits before tax. The same Act, now amended, also required a statement of the value of goods exported.

The current legislation (CA 1981) has moved in the direction of more disclosure and the analysis of turnover by (a) class of business and (b) geographical market, is required "where, in the opinion of the directors, there is more than one class and/or market". The profit or loss before taxation attributable to each class of business is also required. In view of the normal emphasis elsewhere on the "bottom line" the emphasis on profit before taxation is unusual. Information related to employees and employment costs (number employed in different locations/countries and the aggregate cost of wages and salaries, social security costs, pensions) is also required. There is no UK accounting standard on the subject of segmented accounts and it has recently been taken off the programme although a research study paper was prepared by Coopers & Lybrand (1977). The Stock Exchange in London states in its guidance notes for quoted companies, that shareholders should be made aware of significant contributions to the financial results (turnover and trading results) of the company derived from activities carried out in any territories outside the UK. There are other guidance notes as to what percentages of sales and/or profits need to arise overseas, and in a particular area before information needs to be given. "The regulations have been interpreted by management in a variety of ways" (Gray and Radebaugh 1981).

The EEC Fourth Directive, which applied to individual companies, rather than the consolidated accounts of groups of companies, requires sales revenue to be broken down into geographical markets in so far as the scale of activities of the companies substantially differ from one market to another. The Seventh Directive, which relates to group accounts, requires a geographical breakdown of activities, with in addition a division shown between the internal trading of the company and its sales to external customers.

The IASC standard No. 14 requires disclosure of the following financial information for each reported industry and geographical segment:

(a) sales or other operating revenues, distinguishing between revenue derived from customers outside the enterprise and revenue derived from other segments,

(b) segment result,

(c) segment assets employed, expressed either in monetary amounts or as percentages of the consolidated totals, and,

(d) the basis of inter-segment pricing.

This is not greater disclosure than required by FASB 14, but it would require more disclosure than that currently required of UK companies. When the Accounting Standards Committee (UK and Ireland) published the International Standard to its members, the preface reminded readers that "they do not override UK and Irish law and SSAPs", and drew attention to the additional matters, (a), (c) and (d) in the international standard.

The reference to inter-segment pricing also reflects the interest of inter-governmental bodies with international accounting. The UN 1977 draft guidelines have recommendations on details that should be disclosed, and the OECD guidelines (1976) recommend the disclosure of investment and employees by geographical areas as well as that of sales and profits.

Gray and Radebaugh (1981) conducted an empirical study into the segmented geographical disclosure of a number of US based and UK based multinational companies. They differentiate between the information given in the annual report, in the general business narrative, and in the notes to the financial statements. In both places information can be given relating to international operations. In the first of these places, in what might be called the qualitative sections, the UK companies do provide more to inform shareholders than do the USA companies. When it comes to the quantitative sections, that is, the notes to the accounts, it is the US companies who disclose the more information. The standards in the US are more demanding. The research does show that the US companies do tend to divide the world into smaller segments than do UK companies. Nevertheless there is still room for improvement. Arnold et al (1980) are critical with regard to the level of segment disclosure by US companies. They found that a great deal of diversity exists in regard to disclosure of foreign activities. There being a tendency not to disclose foreign activities at the subcontinent or country level.

Fisher (1980) and Bavishi and Wyman (1980) also found that the definition of geographical areas employed by US and European companies were often arbitrary and lacking in information content.

Emmanuel and Gray (1978) found that financial analysts in the UK regarded segmented disclosure as being of prime importance with regard to meaningful disclosure. The Corporate Report (1975) also drew attention to the importance of disaggregated information. The idea of segmented disclosure undoubtedly has appeal. Does it really have any practical usefulness? Kinney (1971), Collins (1976) and Emmanuel and Pick (1980) in papers concerned with the prediction of company earnings, have all concluded that not surprisingly predictions based on disaggregated data, that is segmented data, are more accurate than predictions based on aggregated data. These particular studies were referring to a breakdown of data into industrial segments. Such industrial segmented information is available and so it is possible to undertake research to ascertain if segmented data is better for forecasting purposes than aggregated data. There is not sufficient geographically segmented data available on a meaningful and consistent basis to enable researchers to test whether details of the geographic distribution of assets, sales and earnings enable better predictions to be made than from aggregated data. This point is discussed by Gray and Radebaugh (1981).

c) Management Information Systems and Control

It can be argued that one of the most important aspects of international accounting has received the least attention in the literature. It is possible that the most fruitful area for international cooperation in the 1980's, and the area of accounting in which the spread of ideas would be of most benefit to developing countries would be in the management accounting area. The professional firms are not as involved in this area of the subject as in financial accounting, so less has been written and published by them on this subject. The Berg et al (1969) book of readings, possibly because of limited space, does not include any article on Management Accounting. However the work of the members of the AAA's Committee on International Accounting, and others, meant that Choi and Mueller (1979) considered it desirable. They were able to include fifteen articles in the section on managerial accounting issues. With the usual imprecise accounting terminology, 'managerial' is not necessarily identical to 'management'. Bedford (1976) and Enthoven (1982) argue this is a most important area for the point of view of decision making, and one that is most important for economic development. The topics that could have important implications for multinational corporations include budgeting, planning and control, transfer pricing, performance measurement and evaluation, investment appraisal and subsequent audit, internal audit and management information systems generally. The IFAC have an International Management Accounting Committee, which has issued a number of guidelines on the roles and responsibilities of the Management Accountant. These have been aimed at an international audience.

The 12th International Congress of Accountants had six papers presented to it concerned with Management Accounting. The theme of these papers was the changing role of the Management Accountant. It reflects a changing interest as earlier congresses placed less emphasis on management accounting. Two of the papers were on the subject of "Management Accountants' Leadership Responsibilities to Society" (Taylor 1982, Castillo 1982). The emphasis was on the increasing social responsibility of business and the relevance of this to the management accountants traditional role of identifying the important issues and measuring the relevant factors. The papers at first sight appear to be more concerned with the newly identified needs of developing countries, than with improving the management accounting process in developed countries. It is possible, however, that the two go together. A survey of social responsibility disclosure in the USA indicates that many items now shown in the annual reports of the largest US corporations may be similar to what needs to be disclosed in the accounts of companies in developing countries; for example, information on the business operations with regard to the environment, energy usage, fair business practices, employee health, safety and training. (See Beresford and Segal 1979.)

Enthoven (1982) calls for "an international management accounting theory". This would differ from such theories of a more national nature, because the conceptual framework would be different due to different objectives. The international demands would give the theory "an extra-dimensional nature". This would be due to the need in many environments for national and micro cost-benefit measures, the need to measure externalities, and the need with multinationaloperations to develop value added statements, social indicators and uniform classification. Enthoven gives details of the educational and research implications of international management accounting.

i) Budgeting, planning and control and management information systems generally.

As well as the developing country aspects of management accounting, there are also problems that arise from planning and controlling a large multinational business. This has also received less attention in the literature than the financial accounting problems.

Morgan (1967) discusses the need for reliable information systems in multinational enterprises and in particular Caterpillar's policy with regard to such issues as 'make or buy'. He explains that the same policies are expected to apply to all the subsidiaries in whatever country they have been established. Problems can be caused however when the accounting measures and reliability of the figures can differ from one country to another. He believes this is a particular problem in cost accounting and budgeting "because of the unequal development of these fields throughout the world". The type of accounting control procedures can logically be expected to follow the type of organisational policy, and Perlmutter (1969) with his classification into ethnocentric, polycentric and geocentric varieties provided a structure for the emergence of "control systems which reflect cultural and organisational differences". The AAA's Committee on International Accounting produced a report reprinted in 1973 as "An Introduction to Financial Control and Reporting in Multinational Enterprises" edited by G.M. Scott. He concludes: "management accountants as information specialists internal to the firm are in an excellent position to assist in developing and implementing information systems which will aid in resolving many dilemmas currently confronting international financial executives". More recently Pascale and Athos (1981) have contrasted the traditional American view as represented by Geneen at ITT with the Japanese approach of Matsushita. Although both were similar on the 'hard' variables of strategy, structure and systems, the major differences arose in the 'softer' but still important variables of skills, style and superordinate goals.

ii) Performance Measurement and Evaluation

The practices of management and multinational companies in evaluating their performance has been studied by, amongst others, Morsicato and Radebaugh (1979).

Perhaps it is natural for accountants to think that their work is more important than it is. Certainly performance evaluation is often based upon accounting style reports. Hopwood (1972) was investigating the use of accounting data for performance evaluation and identified three sub categories:

> "(1) a relative neglect of the accounting data where the data are potentially relevant to assessing performance and managing the task.
>
> (2) a relative neglect of the accounting data where the data are not very useful for assessing performance and managing the task
>
> (3) a relative neglect of the accounting data in performance evaluation but a use of the data in decision making and less evaluative feedback, where the data are relevant".

It is not difficult to see the value of these sub-categories when considering the performance of overseas subsidiaries and/or their managers. The assessment of what was relevant, or controllable, is more difficult.

Most of the studies cited by Arpan ~~and~~ Radebaugh (1981) indicate that the major measure of performance used by multinationals was ROI and that overseas subsidiaries were evaluated on the same basis as domestic ones. Budgets were also mentioned and it must be the most useful standard of comparison. Morsicato (1980) emphasised the importance of comparison with budget both in the local currency and in the parent country currency. This is one specific illustration of the distinction between controllable and non-controllable factors though the responsibility for the currency exposure risk and management must be clearly defined at the budgeting stage and in respect of particular assets and liabilities.

As in many other areas of accounting there are those, eg. Govindarajan (1984), who have considered the impact of contingency theory in this area. His conclusion that lower environmental uncertainty leads to a more formula based performance evaluation approach has clear consequences in the multinational area.

iii) Transfer Pricing

This is a popular topic for managerial economists, management accountants, taxation experts and politicians - and particularly so in the internattional context.

Initially those interested in managerial economics dominated the accounting literature on the topic. The Abdel-Khalik and Lusk (1974) article makes no specific reference to the international dimension and yet Schulman in his PhD thesis (1966) and (1969) and Dunning (1971) had drawn attention to the possibilities of the manipulation of transfer prices to the benefit of multinational corporations. The profession usually considers the topic under the heading 'related party transactions' and Mason (1979) draws attention to the delay experienced by the AICPA in completing SAS No. 6. But this statement has no particular reference to multinationals. However, the relative lack of publicity was remedied by the representatives in the United Nations of the less developed world.

In 1978 the United Nations published "Dominant positions of market power of transnational corporations. Use of the transfer pricing mechanism". One of the conclusions was that "Decisions on transfer pricing tend to be centralised within the transnational corporation, and appear to be taken at the highest managerial level". It is also apparent that multinationals are increasingly reluctant to disclose or discuss publicly their transfer pricing policies, mainly because of the taxation implications. Hence the need for the 'guidelines' referred to earlier. The UN document makes it very clear by reference to the UK Hoffmann La Roche case that it is not only lesser developed nations that can suffer from the actions of multinational companies.

Schiff (1980) drew attention to the change in American corporation transfer pricing practice caused by FASB 14. One of its requirements was that the transfer price used for public reporting be consistent with the pricing method used internally, and another was the disclosure of the impact of transfer pricing methods other than market prices. The evidence quoted leads to the conclusion that cost based methods have been significantly replaced by the market price method. The article continues with an examination of segment data but in relation to product segments rather than geographical ones.

Mason (1979) reviews six studies of current practice in Canada and the US and Tang (1982) reports on a questionnaire survey to which eighty UK companies responded. Fortyseven ranked the environmental variables in the order of importance for international transfer pricing. However, as Lall (1984) says, "the flurry of policy interest which had been aroused in the early 1970's has died down.... Recently interest has been aroused by the US proposal to impose unitary taxation...". He also concludes that the case of the pharmaceutical industry was exceptional and that the benefits of investment are now more important than the potential abuse of transfer pricing. Certainly "regulation, backed by international co-operative measures, can be useful". For a view from a country occupying the middle ground Saita (1982) provides both a useful general summary and an Italian perspective.

Chapter Six

ACCOUNTING AND ECONOMIC DEVELOPMENT

a) Introduction

The question can be asked as to why the topic of economic development should be included in a survey of the literature on international accounting. Mueller's (1965) definition which is a wide definition, refers to the "inter-relationships of accounting amongst countries". Strictly speaking the topic of an appropriate accounting system for economic development which is a national issue is not covered by this definition. However, it is felt that a brief review of literature on the subject is justified for two reasons. One is because it occupies a considerable amount of the time of international and supra-national accounting committees. The second is because although the accounting system appropriate to a country's development is a national issue, usually the actual system in existence is the result of the spread of ideas across countries.

Jaggi (1973) writes that international accounting cannot afford to ignore the needs of the emerging nations. He points out that accounting scholars and practitioners are increasingly becoming interested in the role of accounting in economic development. His article assesses the usefulness of the research that has been undertaken in the field up to that time.

The accounting literature is concerned with two aspects of this problem, one being a concern with such questions as: what type of accounting systems are needed in developing countries, what information is required and are the accounting standards which are appropriate to developed countries those needed in developing countries. The second aspect of the problem is the training required for accountants in developing countries and the means of increasing the number of trained accountants in these countries.

b) Need for Accounting Information

One difficulty in many developing countries is the lack of adequate and reliable information upon which to base decisions concerning the allocation of scarce resources. Accounting as part of the information system has an important role to play in the economic development process. Improved accounting information resulting partly from the improved education and training of accountants could facilitate the planning process by enabling the economic planners to formulate their models on relevant and reliable data. Reliable accounting information also facilitates decision-making at the micro-level, leading to a more efficient utilisation of resources within a firm.

Enthoven has done perhaps more than any other writer to draw attention to the role of accounting in economic development and to the importance of an accounting education relevant to domestic needs. (1965, 1967, 1969, 1970, 1977, 1981). He believes that there is a danger that accounting is normally thought of only as it applies to businesses, to enterprises. There are however two other very important aspects of accounting, namely the use of accounting systems in respect of government activities and their use in national planning activities. In developing countries where the private sector is often small and of less importance than state owned activities, these other two aspects of accounting can be and often are of more importance than the financial and management accounting problems of private enterprises.

Enthoven believes "accounting in developing countries is faced with a series of technical, educational and operational problems, in addition to socio-economic and behavioral ones. The accounting weaknesses in these countries' accountancy systems can be largely traced to historical cultural and educational factors. The significance and function of accounting and auditing in all sectors of the economy is not (yet) sufficiently recognised and in many countries has a low status".

Enthoven (1982) pointed out at the Fifth International Conference on Accounting Education that "our concerns should not only be with the development of a financial accounting theory and framework" but also with the development of concepts, standards and methods of management accounting and government accounting. He believes that certain of these concepts and standards may have to vary from one economic environment to another "as the objectives of accounting may diverge".

The problems of enterprise accounting and governmental accounting were discussed at the 1976 meeting of the Society for International Development. A number of examples were quoted where the accounting systems in particular developing countries were inadequate for the needs. The accounting systems did not satisfy the user groups.

The information available within a business is important from an economic planning point of view. National income accounts which are used for planning purposes, rely on information provided from individual firms. If the information within a firm is inadequate, not only will incorrect decisions be made at the level of the firm, but also at the national level. The degree of usefulness in a particular country of such economic techniques as input output analysis will be governed by the level of accuracy of the accounting information. (Richards 1960).

Mfandaidza Hove (1982), a Zimbabwean with a British accounting qualification, has argued "The way accountancy is practised in most less developed countries is perhaps one of the most important causes of failure to meet social objectives. Because most of the accounting practices currently in use in these countries originated from developed countries, and were imposed in unmodified form, they are inappropriate. This has meant decisions based on incomplete, and quite possible wrong information in some cases, have been made by the governments of the less developed countries. As a result, the policies chosen have not led to the achievement of the desired objective. This situation has continued to prevail even after the former colonies gained political independence".

Qureshi (1975) states that "the relevance of financial reporting to economic development with social justice, cannot be over-emphasised, especially in a developing country like Pakistan". At the first stage in the investment decision process, the credibility of the financial reports is the basis of investors' confidence and so their decisions on what to do with their savings. At a later stage it is the financial reports that are indicators of the success or otherwise of the enterprises and the management ability. Qureshi found many deficiencies in the financial reports in Pakistan. His paper shows that whereas some of the needs of reports in LDCs are the same as in developed countries, there are also many differences. Belkaoui (1974) writes about a class elite, in many developing countries, who are interested in maintaining secrecy. Without a reliable system of financial reporting it is easy for this elite to maintain secrecy for their own gain.

Unfortunately there is no single path to economic development that can be followed by all countries. An economic model that might be workable in one situation might be quite inappropriate in another situation despite some similarities in the two environments. The process of economic development, therefore, involves determining the necessary economic inputs that will produce the required products or outputs. Developing accurate and reliable data and accounting information that will facilitate the planning process will not be an easy exercise (See Morgenstern, 1963 and Kosiol 1969). Apart from the accuracy and reliability of the information system, the manner in which it is presented may affect its usefulness for planning purposes.

At the micro-level the accounting function in developing countries should not be limited to a stewardship and reporting role, but should include all related aspects of operating decisions such as income measurement and budgeting and forecasting. As Scott (1970) puts it, "Accounting information as the major form of information in a firm, must increase in quantity and sophistication as the business environment becomes more complex ..... (In addition) accountants should be more than mere collectors of information and preparers of reports". If this is what is demanded from the accounting information in order to fulfil the planning needs of developing countries, then it is quite imperative that "accounting education and training ... should be accorded an urgency at least equal to that of technological education and training" (Mahon 1973).

At the macro level the increasing entrepreneurial role played by governments of developing countries at local and national level creates more demand for adequate information not only for planning purposes, but also for controlling the economy as a whole. All government economic development activities should be based on well-informed decision making. This again emphasises the role of accounting in assisting decision-makers to arrive at sound decisions.

Puxty, Oliga and Chua (1981) indicate a possible problem. They point to the fact that in the majority of developing countries, accounting education and practice are modelled on criteria relevant to industrialised countries. Those criteria are based upon the pre-eminence of capital in all its modes and its relations with production. It is argued that such criteria are necessarily imbued with capitalist ideology such that the resulting theories and practices are ideologically pre-determined. This contrasts sharply with the widely held view that accounting can be treated as a technology, devoid of human value presuppositions and whose criterion for effectiveness lies in and is circumscribed by economic 'rationality'. Puxty et al believe that many Third World countries have now recognised that development strategies modelled on industrial countries are not appropriate to their problems and needs. Consequently accounting models based on those of industrialised countries are not likely to be appropriate to LDC's accounting needs.

Unfortunately although it is easy to criticise the accounting models of capitalist based industrialised countries it is not easy to come up with alternative models. This clearly is an area for research.

c) Training Accountants in Developing Countries

A number of accounting bodies in developed countries have concerned themselves with helping to satisfy the accounting needs of developing countries. They have placed an emphasis on improving the training of accountants in developing countries and in increasing the supply of trained accountants. There have been many articles written on the need for providing financial and technical aid to assist accounting in developing countries. Engelman (1962) and Lowe (1967) both argue for financial support. Brookner and Heilman (1960) wrote an article, typical of that being written at the time, suggesting that teaching assistance be provided, and Canning (1968) writes about the selection and training of staff for overseas accounting work. The AAA (1978) published a report of its International Accounting Committee entitled 'Accounting Education and the Third World'. The aim of the report was to develop a greater awareness of the potential role of accounting in economic development and to find means to foster assistance. There have been numerous International Conferences on Accounting Education.

The American Accounting Association have for a long time taken an interest in the training needs of developing countries. The 1973-75 Committee on Accounting in Developing Countries was charged with recommending how the Association should participate in efforts to improve accounting in developing countries. The Committee begins its report by stating that "For decades there have been suggestions that co-operative effort would be useful to foster the improvement of accounting in developing countries. The suggested programs have varied widely in size, scope and nature, reflecting the perspectives, interests, and competence of the one or the few individuals involved. Several have been implemented, with varying degrees of success. However, no broadly based or extensive analysis has previously been made to determine which forms of international cooperation would contribute most to the improvement of accounting in developing countries".

The Committee undertook a study with the object of determining (a) what the accounting practice and education problems were in developing countries, (b) the importance of each of these problems relative to each other, and (c) for accounting education problems only, the preferred forms of international cooperation for assisting with these problems.

Amongst the general conclusions arrived at as a result of the analysis were that many of the most important accounting practice problems are believed to result from causes deeply rooted in accounting education "The study provides support for the proposition that international cooperation in development of accounting education in developing nations can directly help alleviate accounting education problems and can derivatively influence accounting practice problems".

To anyone familiar with the problems of developing countries, the research did not reveal anything new. Its importance, however, was that it drew attention of a wide audience to the particular accounting problems of developing countries. It made it clear that these problems were different to those of developed countries. Whereas to the accountants of the US and the UK, the main concern may have been how to adjust accounts to allow for the effects of inflation, the main concern of accountants in developing countries had much more to do with the lack of internal control systems and the lack of good auditing standards.

The AAA (1976-78) Committee on International Accounting Operations and Education continued to examine the needs for accountancy education in socio-economic development. In a study they produced on the subject (1978), they aimed to

"(a) Set forth a conceptual and pragmatic framework for enhancing accounting knowledge, education and practices in Third World economies,

(b) to assess the role of educational institutions throughout the world in disseminating accounting know-how and expertise for developing economies, and,

(c) to suggest how assistance may be given to Third World countries by way of effective educational training, and research programs in conjunction with local, regional, and international educational, institutional and development bodies".

The main part of this 1978 study was a country by country appraisal of specific accounting needs. The countries examined were Egypt, Malaysia, Mexico, Pakistan and Tanzania. These "assessments were pursued in close coordination with accounting educators in these countries and viewed by the people in these countries". The individual case study approach is important. It is based on the recognition that "accounting systems operate within the socio-economic framework" of a country. Because these frameworks differ, accounting needs and hence accounting education may need to differ.

The ultimate aim of the AAA study was to develop a greater awareness of the role of accounting in economic development, and to find ways of fostering assistance. The Committee believed that the association could play a part by providing assistance in developing countries educational efforts and by helping to prepare accounting requirement studies for individual countries.

They proposed the creation of an "International Association for the Advancement of Accounting Education". It was recognised that this new international accounting would have to concern itself with issues over a wider area than those covered by the IASC and IFAC. "As accountancy is considered to encompass (a) enterprise, (b) government, and (c) national accounting, which require different focus, it is to be recognised that governmental and public enterprise is of relatively greater significance to Third World countries than to Western (free enterprise) nations. Therefore, the emphasis in education may have to be different".

Although the 1976-78 Committee proposed forming another international body, specifically involved with education, the 1980-81 AAA Committee on international accounting did not see that "real benefits could be identified as flowing from yet another international accounting organisation". It was felt that what was needed was to strengthen the international interests within the AAA while liaising with the already numerous regional and international accounting bodies. Enthoven, a member of the Committee, recorded a dissenting opinion.

The politics relating to international accounting is clearly very strong, not only at the UN, the OECD and the IASC, but also at the professional and academic level. Certain of the UK professional bodies are very involved with exporting qualifications. At the academic level the differences in opinion within the AAA commented on above illustrate a problem. The fifth International Conference on Accounting Education met in Mexico in 1982. One of its purposes was to explore how to overcome the problems and proceed with more appropriate educational models in the different socio-economic environments of the world.

Over the years, numerous writers have pointed to the need for a systematic accounting education relevant to the particular needs of developing countries. Englemann, as long ago as 1962, pointed to the need for a flexible programme of education, flexible to allow for individual country circumstances, which will almost certainly differ from the educational ideas applied in developing countries. He believed the prerequisites of a successful accounting profession in developing countries were:

(a) a full comprehension of accounting goals over and above the mere recording of cash in and cash out;

(b) understanding of the role of accounting for management purposes;

(c) recognition of the principles of business economics;

(d) acknowledgement of the public responsibilities involved in the profession.

He points to one particular problem, namely that many native born accountants either have been trained in accounting in developed countries or they study in their own country, but for the examinations of a professional body in a developed country. As a result they are more familiar with the needs of a system in another country, than that of their own country. For a more recent discussion on the education needs of developing countries see Levievre and Levievre (1978).

Salas (1967) points to another problem, namely that students in developing countries often have to use textbooks which have been written for students in another country. Textbooks written in the USA are translated into Spanish for use in South America but unfortunately they are often straight translations and no attempt is made to clarify those US practices which are different in Latin America.

Enthoven (1982) presented a comprehensive paper on the accounting education requirements of developing countries. He repeated the call for an "International Association for Accounting Development", catering in particular for accounting needs of Third World countries in the areas of education, training, research and the exchange of information.

The history of certain national professional accounting bodies indicates their concern with training accountants in developing countries. Such bodies have for many years examined students from developing countries, and have helped to set up professional bodies in numerous countries. Traditionally however, they have based their examinations on the accounting needs of the country in which the professional body is based.

The relationship of certain of the English based professional bodies to overseas countries will briefly be mentioned to illustrate the changes that are taking place. The Institute of Chartered Accountants in England and Wales founded in 1880, have always had a policy of insisting that professional training must be undertaken in the UK. This was a constraint in the Institute's overseas activities. It meant that members, having qualified, could set up in overseas countries, but that qualifications (as opposed to people could) not be exported. The examinations could not be taken outside the UK. The ICAEW did however help to establish and maintain an affiliated society relationship with the profession in a number of countries. The Society of Incorporated Auditors and Accountants founded in 1885 (amalgamated with ICAEW in 1957) had a vigorous overseas policy oriented to increase its membership and expanding its organisation in such a way as to create a widely based professional body. For discussion on the history of these professional bodies' accounting links with overseas countries, see Johnson and Caygill (1971).

Since the turn of the century the position has changed. Initially it was the British qualified accountants who moved overseas and helped to establish local professions. As local bodies became established and local nationals took over the leadership of the bodies, the involvement of the UK profession with the training needs of overseas countries began to change. Some of the bodies moved into the exporting of qualifications.

The Association of Certified Accountants is now the most active UK body from the point of view of examining students in overseas countries. They also have a long list of affiliated societies in various countries. The Association, at the end of 1981, had 31,000 registered students resident outside the UK. This was almost one half of their total registered student number. The Association examines in over 80 countries around the world. In a number of countries, the national accountancy body has grown out of a nucleus of Certified Accountants. This has happened in countries in Africa, the Caribbean and the Far East. The Association are currently developing examining methods to suit the needs of particular countries. In a number of countries the Association's entire examination system is operated in the names of both the Association and the respective local institutes. In some countries, for example Hong Kong, the Association's examination papers are used, except that tax and law papers based on the local law and rules may be taken instead of the papers based on the position in the UK.

There is a little known Association of International Accountants which was incorporated in England in 1932. It has, however, failed in the UK to obtain official recognition for its members as approved company auditors, which has been a major barrier to its expansion. It does however examine students in a number of countries.

As can be seen from the above, the training of accountants from developing countries has become very much an international issue. The different needs are being recognised and attempts are being made to meet these needs.

There is still much work that needs to be undertaken into designing accounting systems that will assist in the economic development process.

Chapter Seven

CONCLUSIONS

There is clearly a growing interest in the international aspects of accounting. The number of books and articles on the topic has increased dramatically over the last twenty years, as have the number of University courses on the topic, and the number and size of international conferences. Unfortunately the increasing interest has not yet resulted in a commensurate increase in significant research on the subject. The problems, the issues in international accounting are many. Goodrich (1982) describes the field of international accounting as daunting. As he explains, the problems of mastering the complex accounting system of a single nation state is hard enough, but this is compounded when practices on a global scale are considered.

The issues are important but unfortunately are not easy to tackle. Much has been written about international accounting, but because much of the literature is professional it tends to consist of opinion stating. One must conclude that in general, the rigour of the literature in this area of accounting lags behind that in other areas. There is a need for more research. Hopefully this will come about because of the increasing interest in the subject.

At the national level the accounting standards bodies have looked to academics to produce a conceptual framework as a means for deciding between alternative accounting treatments. At an international level, practioners have also looked to research as a means of reconciling differences (McMonnies 1972). Bedford (1966) in the first edition of the International Journal of Accounting, wrote of the need for research at a theoretical level to develop an international body of accounting thought on fundamental concepts. Bedford felt that unless this was developed, because of language, political and cultural barriers, "the effective transmission of accounting practice would not be possible". Eighteen years later we have international exchanges, we have large international accounting firms, we have international standards, but we do not have significant research on such accounting issues as measurement theory where national, political and cultural factors can influence accounting thought. Previts (1975) refers to Bedford's paper, and mentions that although in the mid-1970's the practitioners approach did dominate, "the success of international uniformity can only come in a lasting sense if it is based on a more scientific approach". He is arguing for a more rigorous approach for reviewing accounting developments.

Mueller (1967) concluded in his early work on the subject, that "even though we have a large amount of descriptive literature about international accounting problems, little has been done on the subject by way of analysis. We must understand why accounting development has gone a number of different routes internationally and where and how these routes interrelate, and the fashions in which they have spawned accounting concepts and practices. Arbitrary institutionalization of some given set of accounting concepts and practices is not an acceptable solution to present problems even if it were done in the name of international accounting uniformity".

Mueller (1979) writing twelve years later on the state of the art of academic research in multinational accounting, comments that such research "lags behind the real world facts and issues with which it deals".

The AAA's 1979-81 International Accounting and Auditing Standards Committee, as its main task, considered those specific accounting and auditing problems that needed to be studied in order to advance the development of international accounting and auditing concepts and standards. They were critical of the range of research that had been undertaken up to that time, in that there were few attempts to create a frame of reference for international accounting research. There have of course been conceptual articles (for example, Needless (1976) and Weinstein et al (1978)) but there have been few attempts to provide a "substantive basis for empirical investigation". There are only a few examples in the international accounting literature of empirical studies which have tested hypotheses. This type of research is of course well developed in the subjects of economics and finance.

Recently a few such empirical studies have appeared (for example, Dukes (1978), Aggarwal (1980), Shank et al (1978), Evans et al (1978) and Morsicato and Radebaugh (1979)).

Jaggi (1973) evaluated the international accounting literature and classified the studies that had appeared into three kinds, (a) descriptive, (b) conceptual, and (c) hypothesis testing. Jaggi was critical of the lack of conceptual research. He believed the conceptual research should "not end with only an understanding of the existing systems of a country. It must proceed further to develop normative models which provide prescriptions for improving those systems". Jaggi quotes as examples of conceptual studies on accounting in developing countries the work of Elliott (1968) and Seidler (1967). Elliott in comparing the accounting systems of a number of Latin American countries, draws conclusions as to which system, in his opinion, is at a most advanced stage, but he did not develop a framework or methodology for comparing the systems.

International accounting undoubtedly offers exciting possibilities for research, but at the moment these possibilities are not being fully realised. We need to get away from articles that tell us how convenient it would be if all countries behaved in the same way. Normative and descriptive articles should not be discounted, they can be useful, but we also need the positive articles. (For a recent discussion on this issue see Watts and Zimmerman (1978) (1979) and Christenson (1983)). Some subjectivity is acceptable, but at the moment, in international accounting, the balance of research is wrong.

Research in international accounting suffers from the lack of an appropriate perspective or frame of reference. What is it one is trying to achieve? How can one examine a particular problem? What subject discipline should be used when examining international accounting issues? Many problems can be looked at a from a behavioural - organisational point of view, or alternatively, they can be looked at from an economic point of view. An example of this latter approach is that of Buckley and O'Sullivan (1980) who examine the growth and development of multinational public accounting firms from the point of view of international economics. The big accounting firms have grown and become increasingly international. As accountants, what can we say about this? We could write descriptive articles showing how this has come about. We could write normative articles saying how, in our opinion, we think that this development is good for the world. But we have difficulties making positive statements about the issue. There are theories on the growth of organisations and businesses in the behavioural literature as well as in the economic literature.

Buckley and O'Sullivan investigate the national, structural and locational aspects of international accounting firms. One of the issues that the theory of direct foreign investment is concerned with is when a firm switches from exporting to establishing a foreign subsidiary. It has been found by Weinstein (1978) that the motivational forces for internationalisation are similar for manufacturing and service firms. The motivating factors leading to United States based public accounting firms expanding into foreign markets include client service, a defensive management strategy, and an offensive management strategy, namely the wish to become known as international and to move into a growth area. The Buckley and O'Sullivan research tests certain hypotheses on an international accounting issue. The hypotheses are based on theories derived from economics. More research of this type would be useful in international accounting.

Jaggi (1973) in his assessment of accounting studies of developing countries, points out that at the time of his writing, little had so far been done in the field: "Intensive and exhaustive research is needed in order to understand the accounting problems of developing countries and to gain insights into the workings of their accounting systems" Since 1973 there have been many descriptive studies of various countries, but little conceptual research or research involving the testing of hypotheses.

The AAA International Accounting Committee for 1982-83 has been asked to come forward with suggested areas of useful research. The 1980-81 Committee named four potentially significant areas. Within each area they focus on sets of questions which they believe have not yet received systematic scholarly attention in the literature on the subject. The four areas are (1) service expansion by the professional accounting firms, (2) setting international accounting standards, (3) service and public sector accounting and (4) financial reporting and disclosure of international business activity.

Not surprisingly they raise many interesting questions connected with international accounting for which we do not know the answers. For example, what is the motivation for and consequences of the movement towards worldwide accounting and auditing standards? Much has been written on these points but there is a lack of empirical research. Have international standards facilitated, or become necessitated, by the growth of multinational accounting firms? Would these standards affect allocational and/or operational efficiency of international financial markets?

The Committee make the point that the task of setting international accounting standards is fraught with economic and political questions which have escaped the serious attention of scholars in accounting. The Committee's report is important as it demonstrates how little we really know about international accounting standards. It admits it raises more questions than it answers.

Before we proceed too far along the road to international standards, some of the fundamental questions raised by AAA Committee have to be seriously considered. By this is meant that research needs to be undertaken to try to obtain answers. The purpose of the Committee's report is to stimulate research of an academic nature. Hopefully, it has done that. It should also cause anxiety in that it reveals so many unanswered questions.

Over the last 20 years there has been a considerable amount of research in the finance area on the impact of accounting information on share (stock) prices. Such work has been reviewed by Gonedes and Dopuch (1974). Chang and Most (1981) take such research into the international accounting area by comparing the extent to which investors in the UK, US, and New Zealand use accounting information when making investment decisions. This type of research should be important to international accounting standards setting, as it attempts to determine if user groups in different countries have the same interests. It is also important to ascertain the relative importance of user groups in different countries.

Pomeranz (1981) draws attention to the fact that the Intra American Accounting Conference have "identified a broad-based set of user information requirements, giving primacy to the assessment of managerial efficiency as a basis to determining tax and social policy". Here is another important area for future research, determining the objectives of the different economic systems, identifying the needs of the different user groups and deciding in what way accounting data can meet these user needs.

In 'A Research Framework for the Eighties' by Choi (1981) there are a number of suggestions for future research. The book contains contributions from a number of authors. Scott refers to his (1980) work on 88 international accounting problems, and expresses the view that a number of these offer promising prospects for future research. Smith and Shalchi are critical of much of the existing research in the international accounting area, which they see as lacking rigorous methodological analysis. Brennan, after surveying the national, regional and international accounting institutions, offers certain research ideas.

There is a need for more research in the control aspects of international accounting. In Chapter One it was suggested that international accounting could be seen as a stratum, a cross section of accounting. This survey has concerntrated on the enterprise-reporting aspect of the subject, because this is the area that has received the most attention in the literature. The control aspect has, however, been mentioned at various points, particularly in Chapter Five. There is certainly a need in developing countries for more emphasis on this aspect.

The need for more interest in management accounting at an international level has been considered. The need for reliable information and control systems arises not only within the multinational business (for example see Scott (1974)), but also within a developing country. Whether we are concerned with a locally owned firm or the subsidiary of a foreign company, improvements in knowledge and teaching of management accounting are needed, in most, if not all, developing countries.

The IFAC have taken on responsibility for harmonising auditing standards. As Stamp and Moonitz (1978) point out, as international accounting standards acquire more authority, it will become increasingly necessary to have a set of international auditing standards collateral to them. Even without international accounting standards, it can be argued international auditing standards are needed - all the arguments that international investors need to understand accounts produced in foreign countries apply equally to understanding the significance and reliability to be attached to audit certificates in foreign countries. The reliance to be placed on an audit certificate affects the confidence of investors. The survey has not covered the literature on this important part of the accounting function.

If we now turn our attention away from research to education and training, we can end on an optimistic note. International questions are now featuring in professional accounting examinations in many countries. Professional bodies in some developed countries are working closely with such bodies in developing countries. International accounting is featuring more and more in university degree courses. The international accounting conferences now have special sessions devoted to education. If fact, the subject of education for the profession raised a great deal of interest at the 1926 International Congress. A paper was presented on the subject by P.E. Spicer, who became known to a great number of accountants and students through his accountancy textbooks.

There are two aspects of the accounting education debate that involve international aspects. One is the actual or perceived training needs of accountants in developing countries and these have been discussed in an earlier chapter. The second aspect is concerned with the training of accountants in any particular country, and a view that is becoming increasingly expressed is that it is necessary to ensure that accountants in one country are aware of the accounting systems that exist in other countries.

Mueller, in 1967, concluded his book with a five point programme of what needed to be done to lead to international accounting receiving the attention it deserved. One of his points was that "institutions of higher learning should begin to place accounting education beyond the national sphere by making clear that only some of the material found in an accounting textbook in the US would be regarded as valid in, for example, Germany. Separate instruction in international dimensions of accounting should be offered".

We now have international accounting courses offered at many universities. The appropriate curriculum for such courses is often written about (Kubin (1973), Dascher et al (1973), Schoenfield (1974)). Seidler (1967) has referred to such courses as ultimate theory courses. More recent studies are those of Burns (1979) and Mintz (1980).

In concluding this review, mention should be made of the fact that a large number of the articles that have been quoted and referred to were published in the International Journal of Accounting Education and Research. This Journal has done a great deal to make accountants more aware of the international dimension of the subject. Up until the founding of the Journal in 1966 there was no real focus of attention in the literature on the international aspects of the subject. Articles did appear from time to time in the academic and professional press, but they had to compete for attention with articles on the many other aspects of the subject. This journal provided a focal point for those interested in international aspects of the subject.

There is a lot to be done at the research level in international accounting. We need, for example, to develop theories, and to test these theories we need to analyse why different countries have different accounting practices, what are the particular characteristics of a country that lead to its particular accounting methods, what causes the differences, what are the common characteristics.

Professional and academic accounting bodies now have international committees. The large professional accounting firms are researching and writing on the topic. Undoubtedly they have carried out a great deal of in-house research to solve problems that they and their clients face in international business. More and more students and academics are interested in the topic. It would appear that it will not be long before the standard of research in international accounting will rise to the level of that in other areas of accounting.

BIBLIOGRAPHY

Abel, R., "A Comparative Simulation of German and United States Accounting Principles", Journal of Accounting Research, Spring 1969.

________, "The impact of environment on Accounting practices: Germany in the thirties", International Journal of Accounting, 7, Fall 1971.

Abu-Jbarah, "A subentity basis for financial reporting by multinational firms: A cluster analysis approach", Doctoral Dissertation 1972, University of Wisconsin, unpublished.

Accountant, The, Vol. CXXXIV (1956), p. 547, London, England.

Accountants International Study Group, "International Financial Reporting", Study No. 11, AISG Toronto, 1975.

Accounting Review, The, Bibliography, 1926-1978.

Accounting Standards Committee, ED 14 (Accounting for Research and Development) London, January 1975.

________________________________, ED 17 (Accounting for Research and Development - Revised) London May 1976.

________________________________, SSAP 13 (Accounting for Research and Development) London, December 1977.

________________________________, SSAP 20 (Foreign Currency Translation) London, April 1983.

________________________________, The Corporate Report, London, 1975.

Agami, A.M., and Kollaritsch, F.P., Annotated International Accounting Bibliography, 1972-1981, American Accounting Association, 1983.

Aggarwal, Raj, "Investment Performance of US Based Multinational Companies: Comments and a Perspective on International Diversification of

Real Assets", Journal of International Business Studies, Spring/Summer 1980, pp. 89-104.

Aharoni, Yair, The Foreign Investment Decision Process, Boston Devision of Research, Harvard Business School, 1966.

Alhashim, D.D., "Regulation of Financial Accounting: An International Perspective", International Journal of Accounting, 15, Fall 1980.

____________ and Garner, S.P., "Postulates for Localized Uniformity in Accounting", Abacus, June 1973.

____________ and Robertson, J.W. (Editors) Accounting for Multinational Enterprises, Indianapolis: Bobbs-Merrill Education Publishing, 1978.

Ameiss, A.P., "Could Swedish Auditing Procedures Result in Greater Corporate Control for US Stockholders?", International Journal of Accounting 5, Spring 1970.

Amer, M.B., "Impact of Public Ownership on the UAR Accounting Profession", International Journal of Accounting 4, Spring 1969.

American Accounting Association, Accounting Education and the Third World, Report of the Committee on International Accounting Operations and Education, 1976-1978, Sarasota, Florida, 1978.

________________________, Committee on International Accounting, Report 1973, Reprinted in G.M. Scott (Editor), An Introduction to Financial Control and Reporting in Multinational Enterprises, University of Texas at Austin, Graduate School of Business, 1973.

________________________, Committee on Accounting in Developing Countries, Report 1973-75, The Accounting Review, Supplement to Volume XLXI, 1976.

________________________, Committee on International Accounting, Report 1974-75, The Accounting Review, Supplement to Volume XLXI, 1976.

________________________, Committee on International Accounting Operations and Education, Report 1975-76, The Accounting Review, Supplement to Volume 52, 1977.

________________________, Committee on International Accounting Operations and Education, Report 1976-78.

Bibliography

American Accounting Association, International Accounting Section, Notable Contributions to the Periodical International Accounting Literature, 1975-78, Sarasota, Florida, 1979.

_______________, Committee on International Accounting and Auditing Standards, Report 1980-81.

American Institute of Certified Public Accountants, Accounting Research Bulletin No. 43, 1953.

_______________, Professional Accounting in 25 countries, New York, AICPA, 1964.

_______________, Professional Accounting in 30 countries, New York, AICPA, 1975.

_______________, Statements on Auditing Standards No. 6, Related Party Transaction, New York, AICPA, 1975.

Aranya, N., "The Influence of Pressure Groups on Financial Statements in Britain", The Evolution of Corporate Financial Reporting, (Ed. T.A. Lee and R.H. Parker), London, Nelson, 1979.

Arnold, J., Holder, W.W. and Mann, M.H., "International Reporting Aspects of Segment Disclosure", International Journal of Accounting, 16, Fall 1980.

Arpan, J.S., and Radebaugh, L.H., International Accounting and Multinational Enterprises, Warren, Gorham and Lamont, 1981.

Arthur Andersen & Co., Accounting Standards for Business Enterprises Throughout the World, Chicago 1974.

Asean Federation of Accountants, AFA in the '80s, Proceedings of 2nd Conference held in Singapore, December 1980, Singapore Society of Accountants, Singapore, 1981.

Baccouchie, M., "The Need for International Accountancy", International Journal of Accounting, 5, Fall 1969.

Backer, M., and McFarland, W.B., External Reporting for Segments of a Business, New York, National Association of Accountants, 1968.

Baer, W., and Beckerman, P., "The Trouble with Index-Linking: Reflections on the Recent Brazilian Experience", World Development, September 1980.

Bailey, D.T., "Accounting in Russia: The European Connection", International Journal of Accounting, 18, Fall 1982.

Bibliography

Bailey, D.T., "European Accounting History" in H.P. Holzer (Editor), International Accounting, Harper and Row, New York 1984.

Baily, H.H., "Some Observations on Accounting in France and Germany", Accounting Review, March 1929.

Baladouni, V., "The Study of Accounting History", Journal of Accounting Research, Spring 1977.

Ballon, R.J., Tomita, I., and Usami, H., Financial Reporting in Japan, Kodansha International, Tokyo 1976.

Barrachin, L., "Theorie de la Comptabilité en Parties Doubles par un Mathematician", 1888.

Barret, M.E., "Accounting for Intercorporate Investments: A Behavior Field Study", Empirical Research in Accounting, Supplement to Vol. 9, Journal of Accounting Research, 1971.

__________, "Annual Report Disclosure: Are American Reports Superior?", Journal of International Business Studies, Fall 1975.

__________, "Financial Reporting Practices: Disclosure and Comprehensiveness in an International Setting", Journal of Accounting Research, Spring 1976.

__________, "The Extent of Disclosure in Annual Reports of Large Companies in Seven Countries", International Journal of Accounting, 12, Spring 1977.

Bavishi, V.B. and Wyman, H.E., "Foreign Operations Disclosures by U.S. Based Multinational Corporations: Are They Adequate?", International Journal of Accounting, Fall 1980.

Baxter, W.T., "Monetary Correction - Adjustments to Inflation in Three South American Countries", Bank of London and South American Review, April 1976.

__________, "Accounting Standards - Boon or Curse?", Accounting and Business Research, Winter 1981.

__________ and Yamey, B., "Theory of Foreign Branch Accounts", Accounting Research, April 1951.

Beazley, G.F., Jnr., "An International Implication for Accounting", International Journal of Accounting, Vol. 3, Spring 1968.

Bedford, N.M., The Role of Accounting in Economic Development, Society for International Development, Washington DC, 1976.

__________, "The International Flow of Accounting Thought", International Journal of Accounting, 1, Spring 1966.

Bibliography

Bedford, N.M. and Gautier, J.P., "An International Analytical Comparison of the Structure and Content of Annual Reports in the European Economic Community, Switzerland and the United States", International Journal of Accounting, Spring 1974.

Beeny, J.H., European Financial Reporting - France, London, Institute of Chartered Accountants in England and Wales, 1976.

____________, European Financial Reporting - Germany, London, Institute of Chartered Accountants in England and Wales, 1976.

Beeny, J.H. and Chastney, J.G., European Financial Reporting - Netherlands, London, Institute of Chartered Accountants in England and Wales, 1978.

Belkaoui, A., "The Role of Accounting in Economic Development: Another Point of View", The Certified Accountant Magazine, November, 1974.

Ben-Sasson, H.H., (Editor), A History of the Jewish People, Weidenfeld and Nicolson, London, 1976.

Benson, H., "The Story of International Accounting Standards", Accountancy, July, 1976.

__________, "Sir Henry Benson Moves on From Coopers", Accountancy, May, 1975.

__________, "A Corporate Report from the UN", Accountancy, May, 1978.

__________, See 'Summary of Discussions' in J.C. Burton (Editor), The International World of Accounting, Arthur Young, 1981.

Benston, G.J., "Public compared to Private Regulation of Corporate Financial Disclosure", Accounting Review, July, 1976.

____________, Corporate Financial Disclosure in the USA: A Comparison and Analysis, D.C. Heath, 1976.

Beresford, D. and Segal, M., "Reporting Corporate Social Responsibility Activities"- XII Interamerica Accounting Conference, Panama, 1979.

Berg, K.B., Mueller, G.G. and Walker, L.M., Readings in International Accounting, Boston, Houghton Mifflin, 1969.

Berry, B.M., "Uniform Accounting in France: Le Plan Comptable", The Accountant, London, 26 Feb, 1949 and 5 March 1949.

Bentley, H.C. and Leonard, R.S., Bibliography of Works on Accounting by American Authors, Vol.2, 1901-1934 With Supplement: Uniform Systems, Boston, 1935.

Bibliography

Boer, G., "Replacement Cost: An Historical Look", Accounting Review, January, 1966.

Boersema, J., "Corporate Reporting in Canada and the US", C.A. Magazine, July, 1981.

Boritz, J.E., "Accounting Standard Setting: From Plato to Robin Hood", C.A. Magazine, June 1982.

Bowles, C.C., "International Accounting: A Challenge for Ingenuity", International Journal of Accounting, 4, Fall 1968.

Brandt, R.F., "One World in Accounting", Journal of Accountancy, July, 1962.

Braudel, P., Capitalism and Material Life, Weidenfeld and Nicolson, London, 1973.

Brennan, W.J. (Editor), The Internationalization of the Accountancy Profession, Toronto: The Canadian Institute of Chartered Accountants, 1979.

____________, "Survey of National, Regional and International Institutions" in F.D.S. Choi (Editor), Multinational Accounting: A Research Framework for the 80's, UMI Research Press, Ann Arbor, Michigan, 1981.

Briston, R.J., "The Evolution of Accounting in Developing Countries", International Journal of Accounting, 14, Fall 1978.

____________ and El-Ashker, A.A., The Egyptian Accounting System - a case study in Western influence, Discussion Paper: University of East Anglia, England, 1982.

Bromwich, M., "The Setting of Accounting Standards: The Contribution of Research", in Bromwich, M., and A. Hopwood (Editors), Essays in British Accounting Research, London, Pitmans 1981.

____________ and Hopwood, A.G. (Editors), Accounting Standards Setting: An International Perspective, London, Pitmans, 1983.

Brookner, L. and Heilman, E., "Technical Assistance in Accounting in Turkey", Accounting Review, January 1960.

Brown, R., A History of Accounting and Accountants, Edinburgh, Jack, 1905, Reprinted by B. Franklin, New York, 1966.

Buckey, J.W. and Buckley M.H., The Accounting Profession, Los Angeles, Melville, 1974.

____________ and O'Sullivan, P., "International Economics: Multinational Accounting Firms", in J.C. Burton (Editor) The International World of Accounting, Arthur Young, 1981.

Burggraaff, J.A., Interview, Reported in World Accounting Report, London, June 1982.

Bibliography

Burggraaff, J.A., "The Case for International Accounting Standards" in S. Weinstein and M.A. Walker (Editors), Annual Accounting Review, Vol. 3, Harwood, New York, 1981.

____________, "The Political Dimensions of Accounting Standards Setting in Europe", in Bromwich and Hopwood (Editors), Accounting Standards Setting..., London, Pitmans, 1983.

Burns, J.M., Accounting Standards and International Finance , American Enterprise Institute for Public Policy Research, Washington DC, 1976.

Burns, J.O., "Transfer Pricing Decisions in U.S. Multinational Corporations", Journal of International Business Studies, Fall 1980.

____________, "A study of International Accounting Education in the USA", International Journal of Accounting, 15, Fall 1979.

Burton, J.C. (Editor), The International World of Accounting: Challenges and Opportunities, 1980 Proceedings of the Arthur Young Professors Roundtable, Arthur Young, 1981.

Bywater, M.F. and Yamey, B.S., Historic Accounting Literature: A Companion Guide, Scholar Press, London, 1982.

Canadian Institute of Chartered Accountants, Financial Reporting in Canada, 13th Edition, Toronto, CICA, 1979.

Canning, R.J., "Selection Training and Placement of Overseas Accounting Personnel", International Journal of Accounting, Fall 1968.

Carey, J.L., "How can Barriers Against International Accounting Practice be Eliminated?", International Journal of Accounting, Fall 1970.

Castillo, L., "Management Accountants Leadership Responsibilities to Society", Proceedings of XII International Congress of Accountants, Mexico City, 1982.

Cerboni, G., Logismographia, 1873.

Chambers, R.J., Journal UEC, 1/1/1972.

____________, "Accounting for Foreign Business", Abacus, Vol. 19, No. 1, June 1983.

Chang, L.S. and Most, K.S., "An International Comparison of Investor Uses of Financial Statements", International Journal of Accounting, Fall 1981.

Chatfield, M. (Editor), Contemporary Studies in the Evolution of Accounting Thought, Dickenson Publishing, Belmont, California 1968.

Chetkovich, M.N., "Unity in Establishing Accounting Standards", International Journal of Accounting, Fall 1972.

Chetkovich, M.N., "The International Federation of Accountants: Its Organisation and Goals", International Journal of Accounting, Fall 1979.

Chevalier, G., "Should Accounting Practices Be Universal?", C.A. Magazine, July 1977.

Choi, F.D.S., "Financial Disclosure and Entry to the European Capital market", Journal of Accounting Research, Autumn 1973.

__________, "Financial Disclosure in Relation to the European Capital Market", International Journal of Accounting, Fall 1973.

__________, "Multinational Financing and Accounting Harmony", Management Accounting, (USA), March 1974.

__________, "European Dislcosure: The Competitive Disclosure Hypothesis", Journal of International Business Studies, Fall 1974.

__________, "Price Level Adjustments and Foreign Currency Translations: Are they Compatible?", International Journal of Accounting, Vol. 11, No. 1, Fall 1975.

__________, "Multinational Challenges for Managerial Accountants", Journal of Contemporary Business, Autumn 1975, Reprinted in AAA's Notable Contribution to the Periodical International Accounting Literature, Sarasota, 1979, and in S.J. Gray, International Accounting and Transnational Decisions, Butterworth, London, 1983.

__________ and Mueller, G.G., Essentials of Multinational Accounting: An Anthology, Ann Arbor, Michigan, 1979.

__________, "ASEAN Federation of Accountants: A new international accounting force", International Journal of Accounting, 15, Fall 1979.

__________, "Primary-Secondary Reporting: A Cross-Cultural Analysis", International Journal of Accounting, Fall 1980.

__________ (Editor), Multinational Accounting: A Research Framework for the Eighties, Ann Arbor, 1981.

__________ and Bavishi, V.B., "Financial Accounting Standards: A Multinational Synthesis and Policy Framework", International Journal of Accounting, Fall 1982.

__________ and Mueller, G.C., An Introduction to Multinational Accounting, Englewood Cliffs, N.J: Prentice-Hall, 1978.

__________ and Mueller, G.C., International Accounting, Englewood N.J., Prentice-Hall 1984.

Bibliography

Choudhury, N., "Aspects of Accounting and Internal Control in India, 4th Century BC", Accounting and Business Research, Spring 1982.

Christenson, C., "The Methodology of Positive Accounting", The Accounting Review, January 1983.

Clark, C., National Income and Outlay , Macmillan, London, 1937.

Coenenberg, A. and Macharzina, K., "Accounting for Price Changes: An Analysis of Current Developments in Germany", Journal of Business Finance and Accounting, Spring 1976.

Coleman, A.R., Shenkir, W.G. and Stone, W.E., "Accounting in Colonial Virginia: A Case Study", Journal of Accountancy, July 1974.

Coleman, R., "Development of Standards in the EEC", in J.C. Burton The International World of Accounting, Arthur Young, 1981.

Collins, L. and Pham, D., "Research into the Processes of Accounting Standards Setting in France", in M. Bromwich and A.G. Hopwood (Editors), Accounting Standards Setting, Pitmans, London, 1983.

Commonwealth Conference of Accountants, Proceedings of 1st Conference, Institute of Chartered Accountants of India, 1975.

Cooper, D.J. and Sherer, M., "Shareholders Interests and the Social Value of Corporate Accounting Reports", Paper presented to the A.U.T.A. - Northern Group Meeting, Birmingham, September, 1981.

Coopers and Lybrand, Analysed Reporting, Institute of Chartered Accountants in England and Wales, London, 1977.

Copeland, M.A., "National Wealth and Income - an Interpretation", Journal of the American Statistical Association, Vol. XXX, No. 190, 1935, pp. 377-86.

____________, "Concepts of National Income", In Studies in Income and Wealth, Vol. 1, pp. 3-63, National Bureau of Economic Research, New York, 1937.

Costohros, G., Accounting in the Golden Age of Greece: A Response to Socioeconomic Changes, Centre for International Research in Accounting, Illinois, 1979.

Couchman, C.B., "Uniform Accounting for Industry", The Journal of Accountancy, November, 1934.

Clapp, C.L., "National Variations in Accounting Principles and Practices", International Journal of Accounting, Fall 1967.

Collins, D.W., "Predicting Earnings with Sub-Entity Data: Some Further Evidence", Journal of Accounting Research, Spring 1976.

Croix, de Ste, "Greek and Roman Accounting", in A.C. Littleton and B.S. Yamey, Studies in the History of Accounting, Sweet and Maxwell, London, and Irwin, Illinois, 1956.

Cummings, J.P. and Chetkovich, M.N., "World Accounting enters a New Era", Journal of Accountancy, April 1978.

DaCosta, R.C., Bourgeois, J.C. and Lawson, W.M., "A Classification of International Financial Accounting Practices", International Journal of Accounting, Spring 1978.

DaCosta, R.C., Fisher, J. and Lawson, W.M., "Linkages in the International Business Community: Accounting Evidence", Journal of International Business Studies, Fall 1980.

Daley, L.A., and Mueller, G.G., "Accounting in the Arena of World Politics", Journal of Accountancy, February 1982.

Dascher, P.E., Smith, C.H. and Strasser, R.G., "Accounting Curriculum Implications of the Multinational Corporation", International Journal of Accounting, Fall 1973.

Davidson, S. and Kohlmeier, J.M., "A measure of the impact of some foreign accounting principles", Journal of Accounting Research, Autumn 1966.

Davidson, I.H. and Westwick, C., Inflation Accounting around the world, Arthur Andersen, 1981.

De Bruyne, D., "Global Standards: A Tower of Babel?", Financial Executive, February 1980.

Deering, J.J., "The Need for Developing International Terminology and Uniform Accounting Practices", in Proceedings of Fourth Conference of Asian and Pacific Accountants, New Delhi, 1965.

Delaporte, R., Methode Rationnelle de la Tenue des Comptes, Encyclopaedie Roret, 1936.

Donaghy, P.J. and Laidler, J., European Financial Reporting: Spain, Institute of Chartered Accountants in England and Wales, London, 1982.

Doupnik, T.S., "Indexation: Brazil's Response to Inflation", International Journal of Accounting, Fall 1982.

Dukes, R.E., An Empirical Investigation of the Effects of Statement of Financial Accounting Standards No. 8 On Security Return Behavior, FASB Research Report, Stamford, Financial Accounting Standards Board, 1978.

Bibliography

Dumarchey, J., La Theorie Positive de la Comptabilité, 1914 and 1933.

Dunning, J.H. (Editor), The Multinational Enterprise, George Allen and Unwin Ltd., 1971.

Eaton, M.G., "Financial Reporting in a Changing Society", Journal of Accountancy, August 1957.

Edey, H.C. and Panitpakdi, P., "British Company Accounting and the Law", in Studies in the History of Accounting, edited by A.C. Littleton and B.S. Yamey, Sweet and Maxwell, 1956.

Eiteman, D.K. and Stonehill, B.I., Multinational Business Finance, Addison Wesley, 2nd edition, 1979.

Elliott, E.L., The nature and stages of accounting development in Latin America, Center for International Education and Research in Accounting, Illinois, 1968.

Elliott, S., Comments made in an Interview - reported in Accountancy, January 1983.

Elmendorff, W., "Co-ordination of the Legal Accounting requirements in various countries of the EEC", Journal UEC, January 1971, pp. 14-19.

Emmanuel, C.R. and Gray, S.J., "Segmental Disclosures and the Segment Identification Problem", Accounting and Business Research, Winter, 1977.

______, "Segmental Disclosures by Multibusiness Multinational Companies: A Proposal", Accounting and Business Research, Summer 1978.

Emmanuel, C.R. and Pick, R.H., "The Predictive Ability of U.K. Segment Reports", Journal of Business Finance and Accounting, Summer 1980.

Engleman, K., "Accounting Problems in Developing Countries", Journal of Accountancy, January 1962.

Enthoven, A.J.H., "Economic Development and Accounting", Journal of Accountancy, August 1965.

______, "Accounting and Development Programming", International Journal of Accounting, Fall 1967.

______, "Accountancy for Economic Development", Finance and Development, September 1969.

______, Accountancy and Economic Development, Amsterdam: North Holland Publishing Co., 1970.

______, "Standardised Accountancy and Economic Development", Finance and Development, March 1973.

______, "The Unity of Accountancy in an International Context", International Journal

of Accounting, Fall 1973.
Enthoven, A.J.H., Accountancy Systems in Third World Economies, Amsterdam: North Holland Co., 1977.
__________, "The Accountant in the Third World", Journal of Accountancy, March 1980.
__________, Accounting Education in Economic Development Management, Amsterdam: North Holland Co., 1981.
__________, "International Management Accounting: its Scope and Standards", International Journal of Accounting, Spring 1982.
__________, "Accounting Education: Its Importance and Requirements (an Economic Development Focus)", paper presented at 5th International Conference on Accounting Education, Mexico, October 1982.
Epps, M.I., "Realistic Accounting Under South American Inflation", Journal of Accountancy, January, 1961.
Ernst and Whinney, Consolidated Accounts in Europe, Financial Times Business Information Ltd., London, 1980.
__________, International Accounting Standards, London, 1981.
__________, Foreign Currency Translation, A comparison of international practices, London, 1983.
Estere, E.H. and Fernandez, Pena, Spanish Accounting in the Past and Present, Glasgow; Strathclyde Convergencies, 1981.
Evans, T.G., Folks, W.R., Jnr. and Jilling, M., The Impact of Statement of Financial Accounting Standards No. 8 on the Foreign Exchange Risk Management Practices of American Multinationals: An Economic Impact Study, FASB Research Report, Stamford, Financial Accounting Standards Board, 1978.
Evans, T.G. and Folks, W.R., Jnr., "SFAS No. 8: Conforming, Coping, Complaining and Correcting", International Journal of Accounting, Fall 1979.
Evans, T.G. and Taylor, M.E., "'Bottom Line Compliance', with the IASC: A Comparative Analysis", International Journal of Accounting, Fall 1982.
Fain, G., "From Basle to Zurich" in Ten Years of UEC, Dusseldorf, 1961.
Falk, H., C.A. Magazine, October 1980.
Fantl, I.L., "The Dilemma of International Accounting", The New Jersey CPA, Spring 1968.

Bibliography

Fantl, I.L., "The Case Against International Uniformity", Management Accounting, May 1971. (reproduced in Management Accounting for Multinational Corporations, National Association of Accountants, New York, 1974).

Farag, S.M., "The Problem of Performance Evaluation in International Accounting", International Journal of Accounting, Fall 1974.

F.A.S.B. Statement No. 2, "Accounting for research and Development Costs", Stamford, Conn., October 1974.

____________ 8, "Accounting for the Translation of Foreign Currency Transactions and Foreign Currency Financial Statements, October 1975.

____________ 14, "Financial reporting for segments of a business enterprise", 1976.

F.A.S.B., "Statement of Financial Accounting Concepts" (SFAC1), Objectives of Financial Reporting by Business Enterprises, November 1978.

F.A.S.B. Statement No.52 "Foreign Currency Translations, December 1981.

Fieldcamp, D., "International Accounting in an Inflationary Economy", International Journal of Accounting, Fall 1968.

Filios, V.P., "Some noteworthv theories from the French and Swiss Tradition in Accounting", Accounting and Business Research, Autumn 1981.

Fisher, A., Financial Times World Survey of Annual Reports, 1980, World Accounting Report, July 1980.

Fisher, I., The Purchasing Power of Money, 1911

Fitzgerald, R.D., "International Harmonization of Accounting and Reporting", International Journal of Accounting, Fall 1981.

____________ and Kelley, E.M., "International Disclosure Standards - the United Nations Position, Journal of Accounting, Auditing and Finance, Fall 1979.

____________, Stickler, A.D. and Watts, T.R. (Editors), International Survey of Accounting Principles and Reporting Practices, Price Waterhouse International, London, 1979.

Fleming, R., "Accounting for Inflation in Brazil", The Accountant's Magazine, February 1974.

____________, "New Concepts in Brazilian Accounting for Inflation", The Accountant's Magazine, April 1979.

Flower, J., "A Price Parity Theory of Translation: A Comment", Accounting and Business Research, Winter 1978.
Foroughi, T.K., "Accounting in Developing Countries before and after Social Crisis: The Case of Iran", International Journal of Accounting, Fall 1981.
Forrester, D.A.R., "German Accounting Principles Applied. A Review Article", Accounting and Business Research, 1983.
________________, "Conventions, Fairs and Truth-Transfers", Discussion Paper, University of Strathclyde, 1984.
Fortune, "Competition comes to Accounting", July 17, 1978.
Frank, W.G., "An Empirical Analysis of International Accounting Principles", Journal of Accounting Research, Autumn, 1979.
Frederiks, P.G.G., "The Regulations for Publication of Annual Accounts", UEC Journal, July, 1974.
Frishkoff, P., "Capitalism and the Development of Bookkeeping: a Reconsideration", International Journal of Accounting, Spring 1970.
Fu, P., "Governmental Accounting in China During The Chou Dynasty (1122 B.C. - 256 B.C.)", Journal of Accounting Research, Spring, 1971.
Fujita, Y., "The Evolution of Financial Reporting in Japan", International Journal of Accounting, 2, Fall 1967.
Gaedeke, R.M., "Selected U.S. Multinational Service Firms in Perspective", Journal of International Business Studies, Spring 1973.
Gaertner, J.F. and Rueschhoff, N., "Cultural Barriers to International Accounting Standards", C.A.Magazine, May 1980.
Gambling, T.E., "Towards a General Theory of Accounting", International Journal of Accounting, 7, Fall 1971.
Garner, S.P. and Hughes, H., Readings on Accounting Development, Arno Press, New York, 1978.
Garnier, P., "Uniform Accounting Systems in France" (Translated by P.J. Oliphant), C.A. Magazine, July 1962.
Garnsey, G., "Holding Companies and Their Published Accounts", The Accountant, London, 6.1.23 and 13.1.23.
Gerboth, D.L., "Research, Intuition and Politics in Accounting Inquiry", Accounting Review, July 1973.

Bibliography

Gonedes, N.J. and Dopuch, N., "Capital Market Equilibrium, Information Production and Selecting Accounting Techniques: Theoretical Framework and Review of Empirical Work", Journal of Accounting Research, Vol. 12, 1974.

Goodrich, P.S., "International Accounting Groups: A Q-Factor Analysis of the 1979 Price-Waterhouse Survey", paper presented to the annual meeting of the American Accounting Association, Boston, 13 August, 1980.

__________, "International Linkages: Political and Accounting Groups", paper presented to the annual meeting of the European Accounting Association, Barcelona, Spain, 14 April, 1981.

__________, "Competing Paradigms in Comparative International Accounting", paper presented to the AUTA Northern Group, Birmingham, 1981.

__________, "A Typology of International Accounting Principles and Policies", AUTA Review, Spring 1982.

Govindarajan, V., "Appropriatness of Accounting Data in performance evaluation: an empirical examination of environmental uncertainty as an intervening variable", Accounting, Organizations and Society, Vol. 9, No. 2, 1981.

Goudeket , A., "An application of replacement value theory", Journal of Accountancy, July, 1960.

Gray, S.J., "Corporate Reporting and Investor Decisions in the EEC: The Comparability Problem", Occasional Paper No. 2, International Centre for Research in Accounting, University of Lancaster, 1974.

__________, "Financial Reporting in the EEC and the International Economy: A Selected Bibliography", Occasional Paper No. 4, International Centre for Research in Accounting, University of Lancaster, U.K., 1974.

__________, "Segment Reporting and EEC Multinationals", Journal of Accounting Research, Autumn, 1978. Reprinted in S.J. Gray, 1983 op cit.

__________, The impact of International Accounting differences from a security-analysis perspective: Some European Evidence", Journal of Accounting research, Vol. 18, No. 1, Spring 1980. Reprinted in S.J. Gray, 1983, op cit.

__________,(Editor), International Accounting and Transnational Decisions, Butterworth, London, 1983.

Gray, S.J. and Coenenberg, A.G. (Editor) EEC Accounting Harmonization: Implementation and Impact of the Fourth Directive, Amsterdam, North Holland Co. 1984.

________ and Radebaugh, L.H., "International Segment Disclosures by Multinational Enterprises: A US-UK Comparative Study", paper presented at annual congress of European Accounting Association, April 1981.

________, Shaw, J.C. and McSweeney, L.B., "Accounting Standards and Multinational Corporations", Journal of International Business Studies, Spring/Summer, 1981.

Grenside, J.P., "British Companies and the Harmonization of EEC Laws", The Accountant, January 4, 1973.

Gruenbaum, G.L., National Income and Outlay in Palestine, 1936, Research Institute of the Jewish Agency for Palestine, Jerusalem, 1941.

Hamilton, A., Book Review in Monthly Review 26 (1798) p. 129. Quoted by B.S. Yamey in the Introduction to: A.C. Littleton and B.S. Yamey, op. cit.

Hatfield, H.R., "Some variation in accounting practices in England, France, Germany and the USA", paper presented to the annual meeting of the American Association of Public Accountants, at San Francisco, September, 1911, published in Journal of Accounting Research, Autumn 1966.

________, "An Historical defense of Bookkeeping", The Journal of Accountancy, April, 1924, reprinted in Studies in Accounting Theory edited by W.T. Baxter and S. Davidson, Homewood, Illinois, Irwin, 1962.

Hauworth, W.P., "Problems in the Development of Worldwide Accounting Standards", International Journal of Accounting, Fall 1973.

________, "A comparison of various international proposals on inflation accounting: a practitioner's view", International Journal of Accounting, Fall 1973.

Hayes, D.J., "The IASC - Recent Developments and Current Problems", International Journal of Accounting, Vol. 16, No. 1, Fall 1980.

________ and Roy C. Nash, "Harmonizing International Accounting Standards and Practices", (Interview), Arthur Young Views, August 1979, pp. 4-5.

Heath, S., "UN Steps Up Standards Effort", Accountancy Age, July 6, 1979.

Hein, L.W., The British Companies Acts and the Practice of Accountancy 1844-1962, Republished by Arno Press, 1978.

Holzer, H.P. and Schonfeld, H.M., "The French Approach to the Post war price level problem", Accounting Review, April, 1963

__________ and Tremblay, D., "Accounting and Economic Development: The Cases of Thailand and Tunisia", International Journal of Accounting, Fall 1973.

Hope, A. and Gray, R., "Power and Policy Making: The Development of an R & D Standard", Journal of Business Finance and Accounting, Winter 1982.

________ and Briggs, J., "Accounting Policy-Making - some lessons from the Deferred Taxation Debate", Accounting and Business Research, Spring 1982.

Hopwood, A.G., "An empirical study of the role of accounting data in performance evaluation", Journal of Accounting Research, Supplement 1972.

Horngren, C.T., "The Marketing of Accounting Standards", Journal of Accountancy, October 1973, pp. 61-66.

__________, "Uses and limitations of a conceptual framework", Journal of Accountancy, April 1981.

Houghton, K.A., European Accounting: An Annotated Bibliography, Bangor: Institute of European Finance, 1979.

Hove, M., "Why accountancy is failing the Third World", Certified Accountant, London, October 1982.

Hsu, T.T., "Recent Business and Accounting Developments in China", International Journal of Accounting, Fall 1981.

Hunziker, A.E., "Commentary to Discussion on International Accounting Challenges", International Journal of Accounting, Fall 1968.

Hussein, M.E., "Translation problems of International Accounting Standards", International Journal of Accounting, Fall 1981.

Ijiri, Y., "The Nature of Accounting Research", in Research Methodology in Accounting, edited by R. Sterling, Scholars, 1972.

International Accounting Standards Committee, Exposure Draft 15, Reporting Financial Information by Segment , March 1980.

IAS 14, Reporting Financial information by Segment, August, 1981.

IAS 21, Accounting for the Effects of Changes in Foreign Exchange Rates, July, 1983.

International Centre for Research in Accounting, International Financial Reporting Standards: Problem and Prospects, Lancaster: University Press/ICRA, 1977.
International Federation of Accountants (IFAC), Exposure Draft on Educational Requirements, 1980.
Jacobsen, L.E., "The ancient Inca empire of Peru and the Double Entry Bookkeeping Concept", Journal of Accounting Research, Autumn 1964.
Jaggi, B.L., "A review of the Accounting Profession in India", International Journal of Accounting, Fall 1970.
__________, "Accounting Studies of Developing Countries: An Assessment", International Journal of Accounting, Fall 1973.
__________, "The impact of the cultural environment on financial disclosures", International Journal of Accounting, Spring 1975.
Jennings, A.K., "International Standards of Accounting and Auditing", Journal of Accountancy, September 1962.
Johnson, T.J. and Caygill, M., "The Development of Accountancy links in the Commonwealth", Accounting and Business Research, Spring 1971.
Jones, G. and Kinfu, J., "Birth of an Accounting Profession: The Ethiopia Experience", International Journal of Accounting, Fall 1971.
Jusodirdjo, U., "The Accounting Profession in Indonesia", in AAA Notable contributions to the periodical International Accounting Literature 1975-78, AAA, Sarasota, 1979.
Kafer, K., "European National Uniform Charts of Accounts", International Journal of Accounting, Vol. 1, No. 1, Fall 1965.
Kanaga, W.S., "International Accounting: The Challenge and the Chances", Journal of Accountancy, November, 1980.
__________, "The Shape of International Accounting in the Decade Ahead", in J.C. Burton (Editor) The International World of Accounting: Challenges and Opportunities, Arthur Young, 1981.
Keister, O.R., "The Mechanics of Mesopotamian Record Keeping", National Association of Accountants Bulletin, February, 1965, reprinted in M. Chatfield (Editor) Contemporary Studies on the Evolution of Accounting Thought, Dickenson, Belmont, 1968.
Kettle, Sir Russell, Deloitte & Co. 1845-1956, Oxford University Press, 1958.

Bibliography

Kinney, William R., "Predicting Earnings: Entity versus Subentity Data", Journal of Accounting Research, Spring 1971.

Kirk, D.J., "Concepts, Consensus, Compromise and Consequences: Their role in standard setting", Journal of Accountancy, April 1981.

Kirkpatrick, J., World Accounting Report, July 1981.

Kitchen, J., "The accounts of British Holding Company Groups: some thoughts on developments in the early years", Accounting and Business Research, 6, Spring 1972.

__________, and Parker, R.H., Accounting Thought and Education: Six English Pioneers, London, Institute of Chartered Accountants in England and Wales, 1980.

Klaassen, J., "An accounting court: The impact of the enterprise chamber in financial reporting in the Netherlands", Accounting Review, April 1980.

Kobrin, S.J., "Evaluation of Noneconomic Environments by American Firms", Journal of International Business Studies, Spring/Summer 1980, p. 41.

Kollaritsh, F.P., "International Accounting Practices", Accounting Review, April 1965.

Kosiol, E.E., "Accounting Models as Bases of Managerial Decisions", International Journal of Accounting, Fall 1969.

Kraayenhof, J., "International Challenge for Accounting", Journal of Accountancy, January 1960.

Kransdorff, A., "OECD to set up Working Party", World Accounting Report, December 1969.

Kubin, K.W., "The changing nature of International Accounting Courses, International Journal of Accounting, Fall 1973.

Kubin, K.W. and Mueller, G.G., A Bibliography of International Accounting, Seattle, University of Washington, 3rd Edition, 1974.

Kuo-Chang, C., "Accountancy Education in the republic of China", International Journal of Accounting, 4, Spring 1969.

Kuhn, T.S., The Structure of Scientific Revolutions, University of Chicago Press, 1970.

Lafferty, M., Accounting in Europe, Woodhead Faulkner, 1975.

__________, See 'Summary of Discussions' in J.C. Burton (Editor), The International World of Accounting, op. cit.

Lafferty, M., Cairns, D. and Carty, J., 100 Major European Companies Report and Accounts, London, Financial Times, 1979.

Lafferty, M. and Cairns, D., Financial Times World Survey of Annual Reports, 1980, Financial Times, London, 1980.

Lall, S.,"Transnationals and the Third World: changing perceptions", National Westminster Bank Quarterly Review, May 1984.

Laughlin, R.C. and Puxty, A.G., "Accounting Regulation: An Alternative Perspective", Discussion Paper, University of Sheffield, England, March 1982.

Leake, P.D., "International Aspects of Accountancy", The Accountant, London, 2nd October, 1926.

Lee, T.A. and Parker, R.H. (Editors), The Evolution of Corporate Financial Reporting, London, Nelson , 1979.

________, "A Brief History of Company Audits: 1840-1940" in The Evolution of Corporate Financial Reporting, Editors T.A. Lee and R.H. Parker, London, Nelson , 1979.

Lee, G.A., "The Florentine Bank Ledger Fragments of 1211: Some New Insights", Journal of Accounting Research, Spring 1973.

Lefebvre, C.J.L., "Development of Belgian Accounting Standards within the EEC framework", International Journal of Accounting, Fall 1981.

Levievre, T. and Levievre, C., "Accounting in the Third World", Journal of Accountancy, January 1978.

Limperg, T., Bedriffseeconomie, Verzameld Werk, translation (Industrial Economy, Collected Works), Kluwer, Deventer, 1964.

Linowes, D.F., "The role of accounting in emerging nations", Journal of Accountancy, January 1969.

Littleton, A.C., Accounting Evolution to 1900, New York, American Institute Publishing Company, 1933.

____________, Directory of Early American Public Accountants, Bureau of Economic and Business Research Bulletin No. 62, Urbana, USA, 1942.

____________ and Yamey, B.S. (Editors), Studies in the History of Accounting, Sweet and Maxwell, London, 1956.

Lorensen, L., "Reporting Foreign Operations of US Companies in US Dollars", Accounting Research Study No. 12, New York: AICPA, 1972, pp. 76-95.

Low, H.D., "Accounting aid for Developing Countries", Accounting Review, April 1967.

Luck, W., "The Impact of International Standards and Other Developments on the German Accounting Profession", International Journal of Accounting, Fall 1982.

Lybrand Newsletter, "Trend to increased financial disclosure: international accounting could have important long range effects on capital market", July/August 1966.

Macrae, E.W., "Impediments to a Free International Market in Accounting and the Effects on International Accounting Firms", in The International World of Accounting: Challenges and Opportunities, J.C. Burton (Editor), Arthur Young, 1981.

Macve, R., A conceptual framework for financial accounting and reporting: the possibilities for an agreed structure, London, Institute of Chartered Accountants in England and Wales, 1981.

Mahon, J.J., "Some observations on World Accounting", Journal of Accountancy, January 1965.

__________, "Ledgers as Much as Lathes", in R.W. Estes (Editor) Accounting and Society, Melville Publishing Co., Los Angeles, 1973.

Martinelli, A., "Notes on the origin of Double entry bookkeeping", Abacus, June 1977.

Mann, E.J., "Management and Industrial Accounting in Western Europe", Accounting Review, April 1956.

Mason, A.K., "International reporting of inventories - Potential impact of IAS 2", The Accountant, October 7th, 1976.

__________, "International Financial Reporting Standards", ICRA Occasional Paper No. 13, International Centre for Research in Accounting, University of Lancaster, 1977.

__________, "The Development of International Financial Reporting Standards", ICRA Occasional Paper No. 17, International Centre for Research in Accounting, University of Lancaster, 1978.

__________, "Related party transactions - a research study", Canadian Institute of Chartered Accountants, 1979.

__________, "The Evolution of International Accounting Standards", in F.D.S. Choi (Editor), Multinational Accounting: A Research Framework for the Eighties, UMI Research Press, Ann Arbor, Michigan 1981.

Mautz, R.K., Financial Reporting by Diversified Companies, New York: Financial Executives' Research Foundation, 1968.
May, R.G. and Sundem, F.L., "Research for Accounting Policy: An Overview", Accounting Review, October, 1976, pp. 747-63
McComb, D., "The International Harmonization of Accounting: A Cultural Dimension", International Journal of Accounting, Fall 1979.
_________, "International Accounting Standards and the EEC Harmonization Program: A Conflict of Disparate Objectives", International Journal of Accounting, 17, Spring 1982.
McLean, A.T., Business and Accounting in Europe, Saxon House, Westmead, UK, 1973.
McKinnon, S.M. in A.D.H. Newham (Editor), Consolidated Accounts - The Seventh EEC Directive, Arthur Young, McClelland Moores & Co., 1983.
McMonnies, P.N., Accountant's Magazine, February, 1972.
Miller, E.L., Accounting Problems of Multinational Enterprises, D.C. Heath, Lexington, Mass., 1979.
Mintz, S.M., "Internationalization and the Accounting Curriculum", International Journal of Accounting, Fall 1980.
Modelski, George (Editor), Transnational corporations and world order , W.H. Freeman and Company, San Francisco 1979.
Morgenstern, O.,On the accuracy of economic observations, Princeton, 2nd Ed., 1963.
Mommen, M., 'Le Plan Comptable International', Brussels, 1961.
Moore, R.M. and Scott, G.M. (Editors), An Introduction to Financial Control and Reporting in Multinational Enterprises, Studies in International Business, University of Texas, 1973.
Morgan, R.A., "The Multinational enterprise and its accounting needs", International Journal of Accounting, Vol. 3, No. 1, Fall 1967.
Morsicato, H.G., "Currency translation and performance evaluation in multinational", Ann Arbor, Michigan, UMI Research Press, 1980.
_________ and Radebaugh, L.H., "International Performance Evaluation of Multinational Enterprise Operations", International Journal of Accounting, Fall 1979.
Most, K.S., "Accounting by the Ancients", The Accountant, May, 1959.
_________, "Uniform Cost Accounting", Gee, London, 1961.

Bibliography

Most, K.S., "Essay on Comparative Accounting", Accountancy, January, 1962.

__________, "How bad are European Accounts?", Accountancy, January, 1964.

__________, "The French Accounting Experience", International Journal of Accounting, Vol. 7, Fall 1971.

__________, "Sombart's propositions revisited", Accounting Review, October, 1972.

Mueller, G.G., "The Dimensions of the International Accounting Problem", Accounting Review, January, 1963.

_____________, "Whys and Hows of International Accounting", Accounting Review, April, 1965.

_____________, "Are Traditional Foreign Exchange Translation Methods Obsolete?", California Management Review, Summer, 1965.

_____________, International Accounting, Macmillan, New York, 1967.

_____________, "Accounting Principles generally accepted in the United States versus those generally accepted elsewhere", International Journal of Accounting, Spring 1968.

_____________, "Academic research in International Accounting", International Journal of Accounting, Fall 1970.

_____________, "International View of Accounting and Disclosure", International Journal of Accounting, Fall 1972.

_____________, "St. Louis to Munich: The Odyssey of the International Congresses of Accountants", International Journal of Accounting, Fall 1979.

_____________, "The State of the Art of Academic Research in Multinational Accounting, in The Internationalization of the Accounting Profession, (W. John Brennan, editor), Toronto: Canadian Institute of Chartered Accountants, 1979.

_____________, "The Race to Set International Standards for Financial Accounting and Reporting", Annals, School of Business Administration, Kobe University, No. 25, 1981.

_____________ and Walker, L.M., "The coming of age of Transnational Financial Reporting", Journal of Accountancy, July 1976.

Mumford, M., "The End of a Familiar Inflation Accounting Cycle", Accounting and Business Research, Spring 1979.

_____________, "An historical defence of Henry Rand Hatfield", Abacus, December 1980.

Mumford, M., "The origins of Consolidated Accounts", paper presented to AUTA - Northern Group, Birmingham, September 1981.

Nair, R.D., "The impact of disclosure and measurement practices on International Accounting Classifications", pp. 426-450, Accounting Review, July 1980, reprinted in S.J. Gray, 1983, op. cit.

__________ and Frank, W.G., "The harmonization of International Accounting Standards 1973-1979", International Journal of Accounting, Fall 1981.

Needles, B.E., "Implementing a Framework for the International Transfer of Accounting Technology", International Journal of Accounting, Fall 1976.

Ng, D., "An Information Economics Analysis of Financial Reporting and External Auditing", Accounting Review, October 1978.

Niehus, R.J., "Generally accepted auditing principles in Germnay", International Journal of Accounting, Vol. 4, No. 2.

Nishikana, K., "The early history of Double Entry Bookkeeping in Japan", in A.C. Littleton and B. Yamey, Studies in the History of Accounting, Sweet and Maxwell, London, 1956.

Nobes, C.W., "Harmonisation of Corporate Accounting and Taxation in the EEC", Certified Accountant, August 1978.

__________, "Harmonisation of Accounting within The European Communities: The Fourth Directive on Company Law", International Journal of Accounting, 15, Spring, 1980, reprinted in S.J. Gray, 1983, op. cit.

__________, "A Review of the Translation Debate", Accounting and Business Research, Autumn 1980, reprinted in S.J. Gray, 1983, op. cit.

__________, "An Empirical Analysis of International Accounting Principles: A Comment", Journal of Accounting Research, Spring 1981.

__________, Review of "International Survey of Accounting Principles and Reporting Practices", Accounting and Business Research, Summer 1981.

__________, "A Judgemental International Classification of Financial Reporting Practices", Journal of Business Finance and Accounting, Spring 1983.

__________ and Matatko, J., "Classification of National Systems of Financial Accounting", AUTA Review, Autumn 1980.

__________ and Parker, R.H., Comparative International Accounting, Philip Allan, Oxford, U.K., 1981.

Ogundele, B., "The accounting profession in Nigeria: an international perspective", International Journal of Accounting, Fall 1969.
Ogura, E., "The Nakai Families Bookkeeping System", Accounting and Business Research, Spring 1982.
Oldham, K.M., Accounting Systems and Practice in Europe, Gower Press, 1975, Epping, Essex.
Organisation for Economic Co-operation and Development, International Investment and Multinational Enterprises, Paris, 1976, revised edition Paris, 1979.
Organisation for Economic Co-operation and Development, Review of the Declarations and Decisions, Paris 1979.
Organisation for Economic Co-Operation and Development, Responsibility of Parent Companies for their Subsidiaries, 1980, Paris.
Organisation for Economic Co-operation and Development, Accounting Practices in OECD Countries, Paris, 1980.
Pacioli, L., Summa de Arithmetica, Geometria Proportione et Proportionalità, 1494, Venice.
Parker, R.H., "Principles and Practice in translating Foreign Currencies", Abacus, December 1970.
____________, "Some International Aspects of Accounting", Journal of Business Finance, Vol. 3, No. 4, 1971, reprinted in S.J. Gray (Editor), International Accounting and Transnational Decisions, Butterworth, London, 1983.
____________, "Concepts of Consolidation in the EEC", Accountancy, February, 1977, reprinted in S.J. Gray, 1983, op. cit.
____________, "Explaining national differences in consolidated accounts", Accounting and Business Research 1977, reprinted in T.A. Lee and R.H. Parker (Editors), The Evolution of Corporate Financial Reporting, Nelson, 1979.
Parker, W.E., "A European Plan of Accounts", Accountancy, October, 1964.
Parkinson, R.M., "Translation of Foreign Currencies", CICA 1972.
Parry, M., "Third World needs a new style of Economic Development Accounting", Certified Accountant, London, December 1982.
Pascale, R.T. and Athos, A.G., The Art of Japanese Management , reprinted by Penguin Books 1982.
Paton, W., Correspondence in Journal of Accountancy, September, 1960.

Patz, D.H., "A Price Parity Theory of Translation", Accounting and Business Research, Winter 1977.

_________, "A Price Parity Theory of Translation: A Reply", Accounting and Business Research, Winter 1978.

_________, "Price Parity Translation: Methodology and Implementation", Accounting and Business Research, Spring 1981.

Peasnell, K.V., "The Function of a conceptual framework for Corporate Financial Reporting", Accounting and Business Research, Autumn, 1982.

Peloubet, M.E., "The Historical Development of Accounting", in Modern Accounting Theory, Editor, M. Backer, Englewood Cliffs, N.J., Prentice-Hall, 1966.

Pendlebury, M.W., An international comparison of Group Accounting, Institute of Chartered Accountants in England and Wales - Research Committee Occasional Paper, No. 16, 1978.

Penndorf, B., Geschichte der Buchhaltung in Deutschland, Leipzig, 1913.

Perera, M.H.B., "Accounting and Its Environment in Sri Lanka", Abacus, June 1975, pp. 86-96.

Perlmutter, H., "The Tortuous Evolution of the Multinational Corporation", Columbia Journal of World Business, Jan/Feb 1969.

Perridon, L., "Harmonization and Verification of Company Accounts in the EEC", Journal UEC, July 1975.

Persen, William and Van Lessig, "Evaluating the Financial Performance of Overseas Operations", New York, 1979, Financial Executives' Research Foundation.

Pixley, F,W., Auditors, Their Duties and Responsibilities, London, 1881.

Pomeranz, F., "Prospects for international accounting and auditing standards - the transnationals in Governmental regulations", International Journal of Accounting, Fall 1981.

Previts, G.J., "On the subject of Methodology and Models for International Accountancy", International Journal of Accounting, Spring 1975.

_________ and Merino, B.D., A History of Accounting in America, John Wiley, New York, 1979.

Price Waterhouse, Accounting principles and reporting practices: a survey in 38 countries, Institute of Chartered Accountants in England and Wales, London, 1973.

_________, Accounting principles and reporting practices: a survey in 46 countries,

Institute of Chartered Accountants in England and Wales, London, 1976.
Price Waterhouse, International Accounting news, London, First issue August 1976.
________________, International Survey of Accounting Principles and Reporting Practices, Butterworth, London, 1980.
Puxty, A.G., Oliga, J.C. and Chua, W.F., "Accounting and Western Imperialism in the Third World", paper presented to the Fourth Annual Conference of the European Accounting Association, Barcelona, 1981.
Queenan, J.W., "Challenges in International Auditing", International Journal of Accounting, Fall 1965.
Qureshi, M.A., "Private Enterpise Accounting and Economic Development in Pakistan", International Journal of Accounting, Spring 1974.
____________, "Economic Development, Social Justice and Financial Reporting", Management International Review, June 1975.
Radebaugh, L.H., "The international dimension of the FASB: Translation and Disclosure of Foreign Operations", International Journal of Accounting, Spring 1974.
________________, "Accounting for price level and exchange rate changes for US international firms: an emprical study", Journal of International Business Studies, Fall 1974.
________________, "Environmental factors influencing the development of accounting objectives, standards and practices in Peru". International Journal of Accounting, Fall 1975.
Rappaport, A. and Lerner, E.M., A Framework for Financial Reporting by Diversified Companies, New York: National Association of Accountants, 1969.

Reydel, A., "Harmonization of Accounting and Auditing Practice in the last 5 years", European Journal of Accounting, January 1978.
Richards, A.B., "Input-Output Accounting for Business", Accounting Review, 35, 1960, pp. 429-436.
Richards, W.R., "Auditing US Companies with Operations Abroad", International Journal of Accounting, Fall 1976.
Riise, A., "Norwegian Standards for Annual Reporting Requirements and Chart of Accounts", International Journal of Accounting, Spring 1982.

Rivera, J., "Latin American Accounting - A General Perspective", International Journal of Accounting, Fall 1969.
de Roover, R., "New perspectives on the history of accounting", Accounting Review, XXX, 1955.
__________, "The development of accounting prior to Luca Pacioli according to the account books of medieval merchants", in Studies in the History of Accounting, A.C. Littleton and B.S. Yamey (Editors), Sweet and Maxwell and Irwin, 1956.
Rorem, C.R., "Replacement Cost in Accounting Valuation", Accounting Review, September 1929.
Rueschhoff, N.G., International Accounting and Financial Reporting, Prager Publishers, 1976.
Runciman, S., Byzantine Civilisation, Methuen, London, 1961.
Ruggles, R., National Income Accounting and Its Relation to Economic Policy, Economic Cooperation Administration, Office of the Special Representative, Paris, 1949.
Rutteman, P., "What role the Groupe d'Etudes?", Accountancy, July 1983.
Sahlgren, K.E., "The work of Non Accounting International Bodies", in W.J. Brennan (Editor), The Internationalization of the Accountancy Profession, CICA, Toronto, 1979.
Salas, C.A., "Accounting Education and Practice in Spanish Latin America", International Journal of Accounting, Vol. 3, No. 1.
Sampson, A., The Money Lenders, Hodder and Stoughton, London, 1981.
Samuels, J.M., "The 1904 Congress of Accountants: National or International?", Accounting Historians'Journal, Spring, 1985.
Samuels, J.M. and Oligà, J., "Accounting Standards in Developing COuntries", International Journal of Accounting, Fall 1982.
Sartori, G., "Concept Misformation in Comparative Politics", in The Practice of Comparative Politics, (Editors) P.G. Lewes and D.C. Potter, Longman, 1973.
Savoie, L.M.,"International Dimensions of Accounting", International Journal of Accounting, Fall 1969.
Scapens, R.W., The treatment of inflation in the published accounts of companies in overseas countries, Institute of Chartered Accountants in England and Wales, 1975.
Schar, J.F.(Editor) Buchhaltung und Bilanz, Berlin 1922.
Schiff, M., "Transfer Pricing for Public Reporting: A case study", Accounting and Business Research, Autumn 1980.

Schmalenbach, E., "Der Kontenrahmen",Leipzig, 1927.

Scmidt, F., "The Importance of Replacement Value", The Accounting Review, Vol. 5, 1930, pp. 235-242.

__________, "Is Appreciation Profit? ", The Accounting Review, December 1931.

Schranz, A., "Modern German Accounting", Accounting Review, June 1930.

__________, "International position of accountancy and business administration", paper presented to International Congress of Accounting, Berlin 1938.

Schulze Sur Wiesch, et. al., European Journal of Accounting, July 1975.

Schybergson, H., "German and American Theories on Accounting", paper presented to International Congress of Accountants, Berlin, 1938.

Scott, D.R., The Cultural Significance of Accounts, Scholars Book Co., Kansas, 1931, reprinted 1973.

Scott, G.M., "Private Enterprise Accounting in Developing Countries", International Journal of Accounting, Fall 1968.

__________, "A Business Economics Foundation for Accounting: The Dutch experience", International Journal of Accounting, Spring 1970.

__________, Accounting and Developing Nations, International Accounting Studies Institute, University of Washington, 1970.

__________, "Information Systems and Coordination in Multinational Enterprises", International Journal of Accounting, Spring 1974.

__________ and Troberg, P., Eighty-Eight International Accounting Problems in rank order of importance - A Delphi Evaluation, American Accounting Association, 1980.

Seidler, L.J., "International Accounting - The Ultimate Theory Course", Accounting Review, October, 1967.

__________, The Function of Accounting in Economic Development: Turkey as a Case Study, Praeger, New York, 1967.

__________, "Teaching business administration overseas: The case for the ugly American", International Journal of Accounting, Fall 1968.

__________, "A comparison of the economic and social status of the accountancy profession in Great Britain and the USA", Accountant's Magazine, September, 1969, pp. 489-500.

__________, "Nationalism and the international transfer of accounting skills", International

Journal of Accounting, Fall 1969.
Seiler, R.E., "Accounting, Information Systems and Underdeveloped Nations", Accounting Review, October, 1966, reprinted in Accounting and Society, R.W. Estes (Editor), Melville, 1973.
Sempier, R.N., "The International Federation of Accountants: Operating Procedures and Current Progress", International Journal of Accounting, Fall, 1979.
Shank, J.K., Dillar, J.F. and Murdock, R.J., Assessing the Economic Impact of FASB No. 8, New York, Financial Executives Research Foundation, 1979.
Shillinglaw, G., "International Comparability of Accounts", Accountancy, February 1966.
Shuaib A. Shuaib, "The Middle East: Accounting in Kuwait", Journal of Accountancy, November 1978.
____________, "Some Aspects of Accounting Regulations in Kuwait", Journal of Contemporary Business, Spring 1981.
Shulman, J.S., "Transfer Pricing in the multinational firms", European Business, January 1969.
Singhvi, S.S., "Characteristics and Implications of Inadequate Disclosure: A Case study of India", International Journal of Accounting, 3, Spring 1968.
Society for International Development, The role of Accountancy in Economic Development, Proceedings of International Seminar, Washington D.C., April, 1976.
Sodhbans, P.S., "Regulations Affecting Accounting", paper presented at International Congress of Accountants, Berlin, Germany, 1938.
Solnik, B.H., "Note on the Validity of the Random Walk for European Stock Prices", Journal of Finance, December 1973.
__________, "The International Pricing of Risk: An Empirical Investigation of the World Capital Market Structure", Journal of Finance, May 1974.
Solomons, D., "Accounting Education: An International Perspective", in The International World of Accounting, J.C. Burton (Editor), Arthur Young, 1981.
__________, "The Politicization of Accounting", Journal of Accountancy, November 1978.
__________, "The Historical Development of Costing", in Studies in Cost Analysis (Editor) D. Solomons, Sweet and Maxwell, 2nd edition, 1968.

Sombart, W., Der Moderne Kapitalismos, Munich, 6th edition, 1924.
Spinosa Cattela, R.C., "An Introduction into Current Cost Accounting and its Application within Philips", in AAA's Notable Contributions to the periodical International Accounting Literature 1975-78, AAA, Sarasota, 1979.
Stamp, E., "Uniformity in International Accounting Standards", Journal of Accountancy, April 1972, pp. 64-67.
________, The Future of Accounting and Auditing Standards, Lancaster, ICRA, 1979.
________, "Accounting standard setting: a new beginning", CA Magazine, September 1980.
________, Corporate Reporting: Its Future Evolution, Canadian ICA Research Report, June 1980.
________, "First step towards a British conceptual framework", Accountancy, March, 1982.
________ and Moonitz, M., International Auditing Standards, Hemel Hempstead, UK., Prentice-Hall, 1978.
Stevin S., Tafalen van Interest, Antwerp, Christoffel Plantijn, 1582.
Stillwell, M., European Financial Reporting: Italy, London, Institute of Chartered Accountants in England and Wales, 1976.
Stone, R., "The International Harmonisation of National Income Accounts", Accounting and Business Research, Winter 1981.
Stone, W.E., "Antecedents to the Accounting Profession", The Accounting Review, April 1969.
Sweeney, H.W., "Effects of inflation on German Accounting", Journal of Accountancy, Vol. 30, July 1927.
__________, "German Inflation Accounting", Journal of Accountancy, February 1928 and Correspondence April 1928.
__________, "Review Article", The Accounting Review, October 1964.
Swieringa, R.J. and Waterhouse, J.H., "Organisational views of transfer pricing", Accounting, Organisations and Society, Vol. 7, No. 2, 1982.
Sycip, W., "Professional Practice in Developing Economies", Journal of Accountancy, January, 1967.
________, "Establishing and Applying standards in diverse economic and social environments", in The International World of Accounting, J.C. Burton (Editor) Arthur Young, 1981.

Tang, R.Y.W., "Environmental variables of multinational transfer pricing: A UK perspective", Journal of Business Finance and Accounting, Vol. 9, No. 2.

__________ and Chan, K.H., "Environmental Variables of International Transfer Pricing: A Japan-United States Comparison", Abacus, June, 1979, pp. 3-12.

Taylor, C.I., "Management Accountants' Leadership Responsibilities to Society", proceedings of XII International Congress of Accountants, Mexico City, 1982.

Ten Have, O., "Simon Stevin of Bruges", in A.C. Littleton and B.S. Yamey, op. cit., 1956.

Teoh, H.Y. and Thong, G., "Another look at corporate social responsibility and reporting: an empirical study in a developing country (Malaysia)", Accounting, Organizations and Society, Vol. 9, No. 2, 1984.

Tokutani, M. and Kawano, M., "A note on the Japanese Social Accounting Literature", Accounting, Organizations and Society, Vol. 3, No.2, 1978.

Thomas, R.D., "The accountants international study group: the first three years", International Journal of Accounting, Fall 1970, and Canadian Chartered Accountancy, September 1971.

__________, "Research", CA Magazine, CICA, Toronto, January, 1975.

__________, "International Accounting Standards", CA Magazine, October, 1977.

__________, "The OECD and International Accounting Standards", CA Magazine, February, 1980.

Tipgos, M.A., "Potential Liabilities in International Accounting Practices", Journal of Accountancy, April, 1981.

Turk, I., "Analysis of Efficiency by means of Interrelated Indicators: A Yugoslav Approach", International Journal of Accounting, Spring 1982.

Tyra, A.I., "Financial disclosure patterns infour European countries", International Journal of Accounting, Spring 1970.

U.E.C., Proceedings of Sixth Congress - Copenhagen, October 1969, U.E.C. Dusseldorf, 1969.

______ Auditing Committee, The Preparation and Audit of Consolidated Financial Statements, Gee & Co., London, 1978.

United Nations, Centre on Transnational Corporations, The CTC Reporter, Vol. 1, No. 8, Spring 1980.

United Nations Centre on Transnational Corporations, Towards International Standardisation of Corporate Accounting and Reporting, New York, UNCTC, 1982.

UNCTAD Secretariat, "Dominant positions of market power of transnational corporations. Use of transfer pricing mechanism". United Nations 1978.

United Nations Centre on Transnational Corporations, "Transnational Corporations in World Development: Third Survey", New York, 1983.

United Nations Economic and Social Council, Some aspects of Corporate Accounting and Reporting of special interest to developing countries", New York: UN, 1976.

____, International Standards of Accounting and Reporting for Transnational Corporations, New York: UN, 1977.

United Nations, "A Manual for Government Accounting", 1969.

______________, "The impact of Multinational Corporations on Development and on International relations", UN, 1974.

______________, "Government Accountancy in Economic Development Management", ST/ESA/SER/E 10, New York, 1977.

UN Statistical Office, A System of National Accounts and Supporting Tables, Studies in Methods, series F., No. 2, UN, New York, 1953; revised 1, 1960; revised 2, 1964.

Van Cleef, "Nationale boekhouding: proeve van een jaaroverzicht Nederland 1938", De Economist, no. 7/8, 1951, pp. 415-24.

__________, "Beteekenis en inviehtung eener nationale boekhouding", De Economist, no. 11, 1941, pp. 608-23.

Van Seventer, A., "The continuity postulate in the Dutch theory of Business Income", International Journal of Accounting, Fall 1968.

Walker, R.G., "An Evaluation of the Information Conveyed by Consolidated Statements", Abacus, Spring 1976, pp. 77-115.

_____________, "International Accounting Compromises: The case of consolidated accounting", Abacus, Vol. 14, December 1978.

Warburton, C., "Accounting methodology in the measurement of national income". In Studies in Income and Wealth, Vol. 1, pp. 67-110, National Bureau of Economic Research, New York, 1937.

Wasserman, M.J., "Accounting Practice in France during the period of monetary inflation (1919-1927)", The Accounting Review, March, 1931.

Watt, G.C. (Editor), Guide for the Reader of Foreign Financial Statements, 2nd Edition, Price Waterhouse, New York, 1975.

__________, Hammer, R.M. and Burge, M., Accounting for the Multinational Corporation, New York: Research Foundation of the Financial Executives Institute, 1977.

Watts, R.L. and Zimmerman, J.L., (1978) "Towards a Positive Theory of the Determination of Accounting Standards", The Accounting Review, Vol. LIII, January, 1978.

______________________________, (1979) "The Demand for and Supply of Accounting Theories: The Market for Excuses", The Accounting Review, Vol. LIV, April 1979.

Webster, N.E., paper presented at the 50th Anniversary Celebrations of the American Institute of Accountants, October 21st, 1937.

Weinstein, A.K., Corsini, L. and Rawliczek, R., "The Big Eight in Europe", International Journal of Accounting, Spring 1978.

Weirich, T.R., Avery, C.G. and Anderson, H.R., "International Accounting: Varying definitions", International Journal of Accounting, Fall 1971.

Whittington, G., Inflation Accounting - an introduction to the debate, Cambridge University Press, 1983.

Wilkinson, T.L., "United States Accounting as viewed by accountants of other countries", International Journal of Accounting, Fall 1965.

Winjum, J.O., "Accounting and the rise of Capitalism: An Accountant's View", Journal of Accounting Research, Autumn, 1971.

____________, The role of Accounting in the Economic Development of England 1500-1750, Centre for International Education and Research in Accounting, University of Illinois, 1972.

World Accounting Report, Editorial, December, 1982, Financial Times, London.

__________________________, January, 1982.

Wu, F.H. and Hackett, D.W., "The Internationalization of US Public Accounting Firms: An Empirical Study", International Journal of Accounting, 13, Spring 1977.

Yamey, B.S., "Introduction to Studies in the History of Accounting", (Editors) Littleton and Yamey, 1956, op. cit.

Bibliography

Yamey, B.S., "Accounting and the Rise of Capitalism: Further notes on a Theme by Sombart", Journal of Accounting Research, Autumn 1964.

__________, "Some topics in the history of Financial Accounting in England 1500-1900". Reprinted in Baxter and Davidson (Editors), Studies in Accounting, 3rd edition, Institute of Chartered Accountants in England and Wales, London, 1977.

__________, (Editor), The Historical Development of Accounting, New York, 1978.

__________, "Some Reflections on the writing of a General History of Accounting", Accounting and Business Research, Spring 1981.

Ympyn , J., Nieuwe Instructie (New Instruction), English Edition, 1547.

Zeff, S., Forging Accounting Principles in Five Countries , Stipes Publishing, Illinois, USA, 1972.

________, "The rise of economic consequences", Journal of Accountancy, December 1978.

________, Paper presented at European Accounting Association meeting 25th March, 1980, Barcelona.

________ and Ovandoz, H., "Inflation Accounting and the Development of Accounting Principles in Chile", The Accountant's Magazine, June 1975, pp. 212-214.

Zimmerman, V.K., Interview, reported in Weirich, Avery and Anderson, 1971, op.cit.

Zund, A., "Endeavours towards the Harmonisation of standards of Accounting and Reporting in the OECD and UNO - A Critical Appraisal", in M. Bromwich and A.G. Hopwood (Editors), Accounting Standards Setting, Pitmans, 1983, London.

INTERNATIONAL ACCOUNTING STANDARDS

1 - Disclosure of Accounting Policies.
2 - Valuation and Presentation of Inventories in the Context of the Historical Cost System.
3 - Consolidated Financial Statements.
4 - Depreciation Accounting.
5 - Information to be Disclosed in Financial Statements.
6* - Accounting Responses to Changing Prices. *(Now superseded by IAS 15).
7 - Statement of Changes in Financial Position.
8 - Unusual and Prior Period Items and Changes in Accounting Policies.
9 - Accounting for Research and Development Activities.
10 - Contingencies and Events Occurring After the Balance Sheet Date.
11 - Accounting for Construction Contracts.
12 - Accounting for Taxes on Income.
13 - Presentation of Current Assets and Current Liabilities.
14 - Reporting Financial Information by Segment.
15 - Information Reflecting the Effects of Changing Prices.
16 - Accounting for Property, Plant and Equipment.
17 - Accounting for Leases.
18 - Revenue Recognition.
19 - Accounting for Retirement Benefits in the Financial Statements of Employers.
20 - Accounting for Government Grants and Disclosure of Government Assistance.
21 - Accounting for the Effects of Changes in Foreign Exchange Rates.
22 - Accounting for Business Combinations.
23 - Capitalisation of Borrowing Costs.
24 - Related Party Disclosures (publication date 1 July, 1984).

ACCOUNTANTS INTERNATIONAL STUDY GROUP PUBLICATIONS

1 - Accounting and Auditing Approaches to Inventories in three Nations (1968).
2 - The Independent Auditor's Reporting Standards in three Nations (1969).
3 - Using the Work and Report of Another Auditor (1969).
4 - Accounting for Corporate Income Taxes (1971).
5 - Reporting by Diversified Companies (1972).
6 - The Funds statement (1973).
7 - Consolidated Financial Statements (1973).
8 - Published Profit Forecasts (1973).
9 - Extraordinary items, Prior Period Adjustments and Changes in Accounting Principles (1974).
10 - Materiality in Accounting (1974).
11 - Accounting for Goodwill (1975).
12 - Interim Financial Reporting (1975).
13 - Going Concern Problems (1975).
14 - Comparative Glossary of Accounting Terms in Canada, the United Kingdom and the United States (1975).
15 - International Financial Reporting (1975).
16 - Independence of Auditors (1977).
17 - Audit Committees.
18 - Accounting for Pension Costs.
19 - Revenue Recognition.
20 - Related Party Transactions.

INDEX

For Product Safety Concerns and Information please contact our EU representative GPSR@taylorandfrancis.com Taylor & Francis Verlag GmbH, Kaufingerstraße 24, 80331 München, Germany